## "The message in this book is probably the most vital message there is for humans to relate to each other and their Creator."

"In over 45 years of ministry to thousands of people all over the world, most of whom were in their twenties, by far the most prevalent need I have encountered is for us to know and believe we are being loved. This includes understanding what is really loving and what is not. In these pages you will find one of the best, boiled down, simple, practical remedies for this love deficit that I have ever seen. The message in this book is probably the most vital message there is for humans to relate to each other and their Creator."

**Dean Sherman**
International Speaker and Author

"I enjoyed reading this book. I liked the flow of the teaching, and the questions at the end of each chapter help the reader process and apply the key points. The choice of stories and the personal testimonies were also very effective. I believe this book will be helpful to both individuals as well as groups involved with basic discipleship."

**Maureen Menard**
Director of Youth With A Mission's International DTS Centre

"Deonn has been a faithful ministry leader for over 20 years. She has a strong teaching gift and regularly teaches in our schools. Her book addresses a very important area in a person's life if they are to function with wholeness and balance in their relationships. The book is concise, clear and well written. I think this generation will find it easy to read and extremely relevant."

**Fran Paris**
Co-Founder and Co-Chairman of Youth With A Mission Tyler, Texas

"I really liked this book. Excellent revelation, personal honesty and vulnerability, and packed with practical Christian common and uncommon sense. I am sure it will help multitudes to experience the reality of God's love in Christ. The principles will assist all ages and stages and statuses of God's people. I constantly use Dr. Gary Chapman's *The Five Love Languages* in my pastoral ministries. I will now incorporate the principles in this book along with his."

**Pastor Thomas Saali**
Senior Pastor – Cornerstone Church, Tyler, Texas

"This book changed my life! It revealed to me how I had spent my whole life trying to find my value in relationships instead of from my Creator. Now every time I'm in a deep conversation with someone who struggles with life issues, I find myself thinking, YOU NEED TO READ Deonn's book! I want everyone I know to discover the truths I learned from *Love Needs*."

**Aaryn Hauptman**
24 yr. old Missionary with Youth With A Mission

# LOVE
# NEEDS

## Getting Them Met
## In The Best Possible Way

Deonn McDowell

LOVE NEEDS
© 2012 by Deonn McDowell

Second Edition: Printed July 2014
Second Edition, Second Printing: May 2018

Published by Sow The Seed Ministries
296 Jared Tyler Rd
Glasgow KY 42141
Printed in the United States of America

Unless otherwise stated, all scripture references quoted are from *The Holy Bible - New American Standard Version* (Nashville, Tennessee: Broadman and Holman Publishers)

Cover Design by Erin Boyd

# Table Of Contents

# Introduction

Have you ever had an "ah ha" moment? It's a second in time when something clicks in your mind and you begin to understand something you never understood before. Some call it an epiphany, and others call it a revelation. Whatever you call it, these moments can change your life forever.

You hold in your hand my understanding of humanity's basic love needs and how God can minister to each one. My journey to these discoveries began with one little "ah ha," and God expanded my understanding from there. I've taught the enclosed principles around the world, and time and again young adults have shared how the message changed them as they received their own "ah ha" moments. The change in them, and a nudging from the Holy Spirit, inspired me to write this for you.

I make one disclaimer. I do not presume to imagine this book will answer every question you've ever had regarding this topic. However, my hope is God will grant you an epiphany or two of your own as you read it. I pray each revelation inspires deeper intimacy with the One who can provide for every love need of your life.

In His love for us,
Deonn

P.S. I highly encourage you to check out the endnotes and discussions for each chapter at the back of the book. I have elaborated on many things I said in the main text, and those extra comments may be helpful.

Note: To protect and respect privacy, I've changed the names of the "players" in several stories shared throughout the book. I've placed an asterisk (*) after the first time I use names I've changed.

Chapter One

# *Ah Ha!*

*"And God saw everything that He had made...and He approved it completely."*
Genesis 1:31, Amplified Bible[1]

The heat and humidity of the East Texas summer overwhelmed me as I stepped out of my air-conditioned car. Heading toward the log-cabin-styled structure we used as a classroom, I noticed tall, beautifully green pine, oak, and juniper trees surrounded the building, looking regal and majestic.

Pausing, I marveled how this picture perfect setting in East Texas accommodated so many wonderful discipleship and outreach training programs. The three-day, short-term outreach training I presently directed had proceeded smoothly to this point. The heat produced the only drawback. I thanked the Lord once again for the genius who invented air-conditioning.

Walking through the door of the classroom, I looked forward to what God would do through the evening. Twelve students had come from all over the country to be trained and taken on outreach to Brazil or Latvia. As I straightened the room, I silently prayed God would minister to each one in a unique way during the class. I had no idea this prayer would soon be answered in my own life in ways I didn't even know I needed.

When all the students and staff arrived, I introduced Barbara as the teacher for the evening. She looked professional and attractive as she walked to the front of the classroom and stood beside the whiteboard. Though in her fifties, her pleasant manner and superb teaching abilities made her classes a favorite with students of all ages. I couldn't wait to hear what she had to say tonight.

"Let's get rid of the tables and put the chairs in a semi-circle," she said in her adorable South African accent.

Hastily, we complied. Then she looked at each person in the semi-circle and paused.

"I'm going to ask you a question, and I want you to think about it for a couple of minutes."

Barbara paused again briefly, as if to build anticipation in her audience. Then she smiled and said, "What is your first memory of feeling loved by someone outside your immediate family?"

"Does it count if it happened just last week?" asked a grinning girl from the other side of the room.

Barbara smiled back. "Some of you will remember something from when you were very young. For others it may be a more recent memory. Try to go with your first thought. We'll give you a couple of minutes to think about it."

Two things surprised me. One, that she'd asked the question at all. It seemed totally random. Two, it surprised me how quickly a memory came to the surface of the often murky memories of my mind.

I saw myself as a four-year-old. It must have been winter because in my mind's eye I wore a coat. After a church service, two teenage girls stood like bookends on either side of me in the sanctuary aisle. One latched on to my right arm and the other grabbed my left arm. They were pulling me back and forth between them while they argued.

"I want to hold her!"

"No, I want to hold her! She's mine!"

"You got to hold her last time!"

On and on they went. I couldn't remember who got the honors. I just remembered feeling abundantly loved. Sitting in a classroom decades later, my heart still warmed thinking about it.

Barbara interrupted the silence. "Now everyone, please share your thoughts with your neighbor."

As I listened to one of the students tell me her story, I became aware of a sense of excitement filling the room. Those doing the telling were animated as they relayed their stories of feeling loved. I didn't know where Barbara was taking us, but the students seemed to be enjoying the ride.

"Okay, let's look up here," Barbara said after several minutes. Pointing to the whiteboard, she asked, "Which of these did you primarily feel in the scenario that came to your mind? If you felt more than one of them, let me know that, too."

Engrossed in our story telling, I hadn't noticed the writing on the board. I looked up to read what she'd written.

> **Accepted** – received, approved of, not rejected.
> **Important (Valued)** – worthy, precious, a sense of feeling like you matter and you are wanted or needed.
> **Secure** – confident of safety, you feel safe to be you.
> **Comforted** – relieved, cheered, supported, given moderate pleasure.[2]

I didn't have to think long about my answer to her question. It leaped off the whiteboard as I read. In that moment of being fought over by those two teenage girls, I felt like the most important person in the whole world. I mattered to them. They must have loved me best of all the little girls in the church or they wouldn't have wanted to hold me. At least that's how I'd felt.

Barbara asked several students to share their stories and what feelings were stirred by the acts of love. Then she looked at us with a smile and pointed to the whiteboard.

"These things are the basic love needs of every human being. God created all of us with the need for acceptance, importance/value, security, and comfort. They are needs. God put them there, and there is nothing wrong with them. It's often the crazy things we do to get them met that causes us so many problems."

Suddenly, it felt like lightning came out of the sky and hit my brain. Though class proceeded around me, I no longer knew what Barbara was saying, and I didn't care. The revelation bolt seared my mind and my thoughts thundered, "God created me with a need to feel important!"

I realized in that second this need I'd always had to feel important in my relationships was a God-created love need. If God put it there, then the need wasn't wrong. It was how I'd gone about trying to meet the need that had been unhealthy.

Analyzing further, I realized not every unhealthy situation in my life was because I tried to fill the importance need. I'd also looked to people and other things to fill the God-given love needs of acceptance, security, and comfort.

Like unwanted guests arriving for dinner without an invitation, a video montage of people and situations from my past flashed through my mind. As the scenes played, I relived in seconds the pain and misery I'd felt over each stupid choice and every broken relationship.

I shook myself free from the feeling of shame about my failures by reminding myself God had forgiven me for every one of those bad choices. What I needed now wasn't to wallow in grief over the past but to figure out the best way not to make the same mistakes.

I prayed in my thoughts, "God, why did you create me with these love needs? If you put them there, you must have had a good reason. How can I get them met without messing up?"

As I asked God those questions, Barbara ended the class. Her main point for the evening escaped me. However, my one little "ah ha" moment set me on a journey of discovery, and I looked forward to what I'd find as I searched for answers.

Little did I know then that what I'd discover would be given to you now. Fasten your seat belt. You're in for quite a ride.

## Questions for Reflection or Discussion

1) What is your first memory of feeling loved by someone outside your immediate family?
2) What feeling (of the four Barbara wrote on the board) did that person's actions generate in you? Why?
3) As you read this chapter, what words or phrase stood out to you the most? Why?

*God of heaven and earth, you saw everything you made and approved it completely. I acknowledge you made me with love needs of acceptance, importance/value, security, and comfort, and they're good, not bad. I ask that you will reveal to me the way you designed for me to best get those love needs met. Help me to see places in my life where I seek to get them met inappropriately, and teach me your ways for my life. In Jesus' name. Amen.*

## Chapter Two

# *First Things First*

*"We want to share with you the love and joy and freedom and light that we already know within ourself.*
*We created you, the human, to be in face-to-face relationship with us, to join our circle of love."*

Papa speaking for the Trinity in The Shack [1]


Wedding showers are primarily thought to be a celebration for women only. However, sometimes the bride and groom are both present. Local friends and family celebrate the upcoming nuptials with gift giving and advice as the two individuals prepare to join their lives as one. Excitement builds in anticipation of the "Big Day." If you ask the couple why they look forward to the wedding, they might say something like:

- All my friends and family will finally get to meet him/her.
- I won't have to leave him/her at the end of the day any more.
- I won't be alone any more.
- I'll finally have someone to partner with me in life.
- We'll be able to fully express our love for each other physically. (Translation: It's finally okay to have sex.)

The joining of two lives as one is exciting. God designed the husband and wife relationship to be the most intimate relationship between human beings. It encompasses aspects of the mate being best friend, lover, and partner in life. However, in the last several years, I've asked dozens of happily married couples if their spouse meets all their love needs. Every single one of them said their spouse did not and could not meet every love need of their life.

Why? If God created the marriage relationship to be the most intimate, special human relationship, why aren't happily married couples having all their love needs met by their spouse? There is only one logical answer: When God created mankind, he never intended for any human to complete them spiritually or emotionally. He created them first and foremost for an individual relationship with him.

I'll go one step further. Scripture convinces me that God created mankind in the first place primarily to expand the circle of relationship enjoyed by the Trinity. He wanted to include us in their circle of love. Our primary created purpose is to enjoy a close relationship with our creator. Everything else we do in life should flow out of this love relationship.

This probably isn't a new concept for some of us, but for others, it boggles the brain. Much of the teaching presented today centers around fulfilling our created purpose through performing good deeds for God. I once heard a pastor declare emphatically from the pulpit that God created us primarily to serve him. We have to go to church, pay our tithes, read our Bible, pray, fast, feed the poor, clothe the naked, do missions, preach the gospel, and on and on and on it went. Where does it stop? Human beings become human doings, and there is little joy in life when that happens.[2]

If God simply wanted servants, he could have made robots to do his bidding. However, all through Scripture we find evidence the primary reason for the creation of mankind was relationship with God.

- He created mankind in his own image with intellect, will, and emotions.[3]
- He put within us a need to love and to be loved.[4]
- The greatest commandment is to love God with all our heart, mind, soul, and strength. Loving our neighbor is supposed to follow loving God.[5]

- God proved his love for all by giving his son. Whoever believes in him has eternal life.[6]
- Eternal life is knowing God (John 17:3). The word translated *know* in this verse is the Greek word "ginosko." It means "knowledge by experience." Eternal life is experiencing God intimately.[7]

God designed humanity to experience a love relationship with him. He desires we look to him to get our love needs met because he knows best how to meet the needs any time, anywhere, and in any situation, without damage. No human can do that. God is our most comprehensive relationship.

## Our Most Comprehensive Relationship

I'm often amazed by God's persistent attempts in Scripture to express how he loves those he created. The authors, inspired by the Holy Spirit, repeatedly convey God's deep love for mankind using words which communicate concepts of close relationship.

- Abraham was called the friend of God.[8]
- Jesus said we are showing him our friendship when we honor him with our love and obedience.[9]
- Proverbs tells us a friend loves at all times. God is our friend because he never stops loving us.[10]
- Jesus referred to God as our father, and Paul and John call us God's children if we receive him.[11]
- Jesus made clear the Holy Spirit came as our comforter/helper, teacher/counselor, and guide.[12]
- Paul said a husband should love his wife the way Christ loves the Church and gave himself for her.[13]

Friend, parent, comforter, helper, teacher, counselor, guide, lover—sounds relationally comprehensive, doesn't it? Let's talk about these descriptions of the Godhead for a couple of minutes.

Friend – What kind of person normally gets the title of friend in our lives? According to Noah Webster, it would be someone we like, respect, and want to hang out with.[14] They usually like, respect, and want to hang out with us, too, or we probably couldn't honestly call them friend—at least not a close friend.

God likes to hang out with us. This thought was first impressed on my mind after reading a book called *He's Taking Me To Glory*. In the first paragraph, the author informed her readers that God likes to ride Honda motorcycles. She declared she knew it because he rode them with her. The first chapter describes her ride in the desert with the Lord and the time they spent together.[15]

I loved it. As a young adult who enjoyed riding motorcycles myself, her story inspired me. It gave me a new appreciation for the God who wants to spend time with me doing things I enjoy.

Sometimes we just need a friend to hang out with. I'm not saying there is anything wrong with spending time with human friends. However, God can meet us as a friend any time, anywhere, and in any situation. No human can do that.

Parent – The parent/child relationship, when experienced as it should be, is one of the most wonderful relationships we have. The sense of security which comes from a parent's protection, provision, nurturing, encouragement, and support is priceless. I know not everyone has enjoyed these things from earthly parents, but God can fill every one of those needs if we'll let him.[16]

Several years ago, I attended a one-year Bible school. I worked the summer before the school started to try to earn as much of the tuition money as possible. However, I only managed to come up with half of what I needed for the year.

In the middle of the year, I received a check for $50 from my friend because I sang in her wedding. I had outreach expenses coming up and tuition money I still owed. I asked God what I should do with the $50.[17]

"Go buy yourself a new pair of tennis shoes," the thought came. I shook my head. Where did that come from? Tennis shoes wasn't one of the options. I informed God I wanted to be responsible and pay my debts. Should I pay on tuition or outreach? His response? "You need new tennis shoes, Deonn. I'm your father, and I can buy you a pair of tennis shoes if I want to."

Had they known my need, I'm sure my earthly parents would have bought me tennis shoes. However, in that moment, God wanted to minister to me with parental love himself, and it was awesome. God can meet us as a loving heavenly parent any time, anywhere, and in any situation. No human can do that.[18]

Helper, comforter, teacher, counselor, guide – Who doesn't need help once in a while? I heard a story about an African pastor traveling by car to a meeting. For whatever reason, his vehicle ran out of fuel in the middle of nowhere. He was miles and miles from human assistance, so he asked the Holy Spirit for help. He heard a whisper in his thoughts, "Urinate in the fuel tank."

The pastor thought about it and decided if Jesus could turn water into wine, certainly he could turn urine into fuel. He obeyed, and it worked. He made it to his destination with no further delays. God can be helper, teacher, guide, and/or comforter, any time, anywhere, and in any situation. No human can do that.

Husbands are to love their wives as Christ loves the church – As I've already stated, the husband and wife relationship is the most intimate of any we can experience with another human. The word picture implies Christ loves his church intimately. Who is the church? Each individual who receives Jesus as Lord is a member of the church, and he loves all of us in our individuality.[19]

In the middle of a few hours of relaxation at a skating rink, I heard the announcer tell us the next song would be a "couples skate." Annoyance surfaced quickly. I'd paid money like everyone else so I could skate, not sit on the sidelines. I muttered something about not needing to be reminded of my state of singleness and made my way toward the sitting area. However, before I could leave the floor, I heard a small voice in my mind say, "Deonn, I'll skate with you."

Happiness immediately filled my heart. I don't know what everyone else thought, but I started skating with Jesus. In my redeemed imagination, I even pictured him beside me on roller skates, gliding around the rink in his long, white robe with a smile on his face. All feelings of loneliness vanished. Many would call that crazy. I call it the lover of my soul ministering to his beloved.

God can touch the deepest places of emotional need any time, anywhere, and in any situation. No human can do that.

God is our most comprehensive relationship. He has access to us all the time, and we have access to him all the time. He loves us more than anyone else can—even a spouse—because he knows:

- All our thoughts and desires.
- Gifts and abilities.
- Experiences of family and culture.
- Everything that happened to us that influences the way we think and feel.
- And all our love needs and how to best meet them in any given moment.[20]

We need to understand that God created us for relationship with him first and foremost. As our most comprehensive relationship, he can and wants to minister to our love needs. Why? Keep reading. We'll find out in the next chapter.

## Questions for Reflection or Discussion

1) Do you have any thought patterns that lean toward seeing God primarily as someone to be served instead of related with? What are they?

2) Which of the descriptions of how God can meet us (friend, parent, helper, comforter, teacher, guide, lover of our soul) is the most difficult for you to believe he can actually fulfill? Why?

3) Which phrase or story in this chapter meant the most to you? Why?

*Lord, I'm so thankful you didn't create me primarily to serve you but to be in face-to-face relationship with you. I know there are things in my thinking and in my life that hinder me from entering into this truth fully, and I'm asking for your help. Please reveal lies I've believed about you, about myself, or about how you feel towards me. I want to learn to focus on relating to you primarily and to allow you to meet me in my places of emotional need. Continue to show me truth, and I pray the truth will set me free to have and to be all you intended for me from my mother's womb. In Jesus' name. Amen.*

# Chapter Three

## *The Giving God*

*"...But God's gift is real life, eternal life, delivered by Jesus our Master."*

Romans 6:23, The Message[1]

I thoroughly enjoy Christmas with my family—especially when the nieces and nephews are around. I remember one Christmas when my niece, Blair, was about two-and-a-half. We'd just seated ourselves in the living room preparing to receive our gifts. Since my dad was videotaping the event, I played Santa.

Early in the proceedings I bent down to give Blair a gift from under the tree. She looked at the present in her hands, raised her cute little blonde head, gazed at me in awe with her sea blue eyes, and with reverence whispered, "For me?"

"Yes, sweetheart, it's for you," I said chuckling.

She beamed excitement as she focused on the package and ripped away the paper. When she saw the multicolored bracelets, she caught her breath and stared at them with a look of wonder and happiness. After getting help to remove the plastic covering, she put the bracelets on her little wrists and proudly displayed them for her mother. Her mom told her how beautiful they were, and Blair glowed. And my heart swelled with joy. Why? Because I'd bought them for her.

Most people I know enjoy receiving gifts. However, it's even more fun giving someone you love something you know they'll like. Love simply longs to give.

God loves to give even more than we do. Scripture tells us good dads don't give stones or snakes to children who ask for bread or fish. It says if we humans know how to give good gifts to our children, how much more will our heavenly father give good gifts to his.²

God fashioned Adam from the dust of the ground, breathed into his nostrils, and the man lived. The Lord created him in his own image with intellect, will, and emotions, and put within him an innate desire for acceptance, value, security, and comfort. Adam walked and talked with God because man was designed to experience relationship with his creator first and foremost.³

I imagine Adam was like a young child looking to his parent as he followed God around Eden. He listened to teaching about the different trees given to him for food and about his responsibility to guard and watch over the garden. Then the Lord brought the animals to Adam to see what he'd name them. Adam must have done a pretty good job because whatever he named them, that's what they were called.⁴

How many gifts from God have been mentioned so far?

- The breath of life
- Intellect
- The ability to choose
- Emotions
- Love needs that help humans realize they can't make it alone
- A place to live
- Food to eat
- A job to do
- Relationship with the creator of the universe

Amazing! What a giving God. But wait. What's this? Something is missing? Scripture reports a suitable helper for Adam was nowhere to be found.⁵

Can you imagine Adam approaching God at this point and saying, "Look, God, I have these needs. I need someone to accept me, value me, give me security, and provide comfort. You do a pretty good job, but I need someone like me. And for crying out loud, I need someone to help with the garden. The animals are nice, but they simply won't do. We just don't click. It's unacceptable. If you love me, you'll do something."

That never happened. The Lord himself declared it wasn't good for man to be alone.[6] He knew what Adam needed long before Adam realized he had a need. God had a plan for multiplication of relationships from the beginning, and he never intended for Adam to be the only human—just the first one. His plan always included the gift of the woman.[7]

God put Adam to sleep, removed one of his ribs, and from the rib he fashioned the woman. When Adam woke up, God brought him a special gift.

What a moment. I can imagine Adam looking first at the woman with wonder and happiness and then at God with awe and reverence and whispering, "For me?" It wouldn't surprise me if God's heart swelled with joy—because I know God takes pleasure in blessing those he loves with gifts far more than I do.

From the very beginning of mankind's existence God demonstrated his loving longing to generously give good gifts to those he created. But we must handle those gifts with care.

## Handle With Care

I once heard a teaching by a woman named Fran Paris. She asked the audience what we believed was the most important word to God in the dictionary. Several tried to come up with the right answer, but none were the one she wanted. She turned to the chalkboard, wrote the word "relationship" in big letters, and declared relationship the most important word to God, in her opinion.

She continued:

> "God wants to give us gifts of relationships. Each one is
> like a flower in a bouquet that he wants to work through
> to help meet our love needs and the needs of others.
> Why? Because of his love for us. But we don't look to the
> gifts to meet our needs, we look to the giver—loving him
> above the gifts he gives us."

Unfortunately, these words didn't become real to me until I'd
already blown it.

Her name was Claire.* I liked her the first moment I met her. Her
sense of humor, intelligence, and love for God inspired me to get
acquainted, and she seemed to enjoy my company, as well. We
had awesome conversations about God, and her honesty and
realness in her prayers warmed my heart. I grew to love her
deeply in a matter of weeks.

Gradually, I started thinking about her all the time. I wondered
where she was and what she was doing. I looked forward to
sharing all the day's happenings with her as soon as we were
together. It seemed she loved being with me just as much as I
loved being with her.

Over time others began to express concern about our friendship.
Because of our intense focus on each other, an air of exclusiveness
surrounded us. Our other friends felt uncomfortable in our
presence. Without either of us realizing it, the relationship
moved from a healthy friendship to an unhealthy one.

Missions trips and holidays at home separated us for several
weeks. We wrote numerous letters back and forth, and then we
both returned to study in the same school. Four or five weeks
later, I had a dream—one of those dreams where you stand
outside the dream and observe yourself doing things.

In the beginning, I watched myself stand in the middle of my
bedroom looking towards the entryway. Two large hands came

through the door, as if a giant were standing outside unable to enter the room fully. The enormous hands held a beautifully wrapped gift.

I knew the hands were God's, and I knew the gift was for me. I saw myself lift the gift from his hands and say, "Thank you, Lord."

A gentle, loving voice spoke clearly, "Handle with care, Deonn."

I observed myself carefully open the package and pull out a dazzling crystal goblet. It appeared delicate and stunningly beautiful. I looked mesmerized by it.

"Oh!" I heard myself exclaim as I watched myself hold it to the light and turn it this way and that. I appeared fascinated by the dazzling rainbow of colors dancing on the walls. "It's amazing, Father. Thank you so much."

The loving voice spoke again, "Handle with care, Deonn."

"Of course," I heard myself whisper as I saw myself turn, fully focused on the treasure in my hand.

I watched myself walk around the room spellbound by the priceless possession I held. Without warning, I suddenly threw the goblet high in the air and giggled delightedly as I caught it.

Watching the scene, I gasped in unbelief. "What do you think you're doing?" I thought.

I then observed myself circling the room again, staring at the goblet, stroking it lovingly, and holding it close to my heart. Abruptly, I tossed my prize up in the air again and deftly rescued it before it hit the ground. A look of joy encompassed my face.

"You idiot, stop it!" I silently screamed. Everything in me wanted to run into the room and remove the gift from my hands to protect it from probable damage. But I couldn't move.

I watched myself again move in circles and continue to study the goblet, admiring its uniqueness. I wanted to cry when I saw myself lob my gift from God upward a third time. I gazed transfixed at the horror and dismay registering on my counterpart's face when the realization hit there would be no catching it this time. My delicate treasure collided with the floor and shattered into a hundred pieces.

I bolted upright in bed. I'd had a dream, but more than a dream. It was my reality, and I knew it.

Besides its obvious message, one other thing stood out as significant. Once I held the gift and told God I'd take care of it, he seemingly didn't exist to me any more. I only had eyes for the gift he'd given and had forgotten who gave it to me in the first place.

Deception is subtle. It never walks up to you and says, "I'm going to blind your eyes now and keep you from seeing the truth of where you're headed." Claire and I loved Jesus and were leaders in our sphere of influence, but we shared an emotionally dependent relationship and didn't know it.

The spirit of deception is sneaky, and none of us is immune to falling into its trap if we don't keep our eyes on Jesus and look to him to meet our love needs. But God loves us too much to let us wander in darkness and deception indefinitely if our hearts are toward him. Eventually, a loving God will bring darkness to light. When he does, will we ignore his warnings and choose to remain in darkness, or will we choose to walk away from darkness into light?

God gives wonderful relationships, good jobs, enjoyable hobbies, and nice possessions because love longs to give. He works through many of those things to help minister to our needs for acceptance, importance, security, and comfort. But as valuable and precious as the gifts are, the giver is much more valuable and precious. When we lose sight of him and focus only on the gift, somebody will get hurt. The one who grieves the most when that happens is God.

## Questions for Reflection or Discussion

1)  Specify one thing (a relationship, a possession, whatever) you knew was a gift from God when you got it. Close your eyes and imagine the first moment you received the gift. Describe how you think God felt when he gave it to you. Is this the first time you've ever thought about how God feels when he gives a gift?

2)  Do you think relationship is the most important word to God? Why or why not?

3)  What part of the "Handle With Care" section stood out to you the most? Why?

*Lord, I acknowledge you are a giving God. Thank you for all your gifts to me—especially for the gift of love with which you give them. You want to give me real life, eternal life, through relationship with Jesus, and I want it. I truly want to experience a deeper friendship with you. I want to look to you and trust you to fulfill every need of my life. And when you give me gifts to help meet those needs, I want to remember to focus primarily on the giver and not the gifts. I don't want to hurt anybody any more, especially you. I can't do all this on my own, though. I desperately need your help, and I'm asking for it right now. In Jesus' name. Amen.*

## Chapter Four

# *To Be Loved, This Is What I Would Do*

*"Much of the misbehavior of children is motivated by the cravings of an empty 'love tank.'*
*...Their misbehavior was a misguided search for the love they did not feel."*
Gary Chapman[1]

God created us with love needs and will generously give us a variety of gifts to help minister to them. However, if we don't fully understand or believe this truth, we will try to get them met through people or things.

I led a ministry team of young adults to university campuses for several years. One drama we performed received rave reviews everywhere. It communicated, in an exaggerated way, of course, some of the ridiculous things humans do to feel accepted, valued, secure, and comforted. We called it "To Be Loved."[2]

The first of six cast members walked on stage. Facing the audience with his hands clasped in front of him, elbows at a horizontal right angle, he would announce seriously, "To be loved, this is what I would do. To be loved, this is what I would do."

Then in a singsong voice, accompanied by ridiculous motions, he said, "I'll work and work and work all day, if 'Good job!' is what you'll say. I'll work and work and work all day, if 'Good job!' is what you'll say."[3]

Ever met this guy? Maybe you are this guy.

Not all over-achieving workaholics work themselves to a frazzle to get the "well done" from the boss. But some people wrap their whole identity in their ability to accomplish greatness in their work realm. They do it for the prestige and praise it brings them. They do it for the acceptance and sense of value they experience. They do it to feel loved.

Please don't misunderstand. The Scriptures make it clear that whatever work our hands find to do we should do with all our hearts as unto the Lord and not unto men.[4] Followers of Jesus should be the best workers in the company. But if we perform with a motive to receive the praise of men instead of to honor God, then perhaps we look to men instead of God to fill our love tank.

Cast member number two entered from stage left. "To be loved, this is what I would do. To be loved, this is what I would do."

"See me, notice me, don't you want to know me? See me, notice me, don't you want to know me?"[5]

Some people are naturally funny, loud, and outgoing. However, have you ever felt at times people tried a little too hard to draw attention to themselves, almost like they want to prove they are worth knowing? Often what you witness is simply immaturity. Much of the time, however, it's someone begging to be accepted and valued—begging to feel loved.

Next, player number three took center stage. "To be loved, this is what I would do. To be loved, this is what I would do."

"I'll drink, I'll smoke, I'll do it till I croak. I'll drink, I'll smoke, I'll do it till I croak."[6]

At eight years old, I puffed my first cigarette. My best friend stole one of her dad's, and we hid behind the old high school building to light up. I knew my parents would bust my little behind if they found out. Why did I do it? To be accepted by my best friend—to feel loved.

Millions of people are chemically addicted to tobacco or alcohol. I'm guessing most started smoking or drinking to feel accepted, to be part of the crowd, to be cool, to feel loved. Then they simply got hooked.

Peer pressure is a powerful thing. We need to understand real love would never encourage us to do things that could destroy us. Those who truly care will understand when we say, "No thanks."

A young man, standing straight and tall, walked on to the stage next and took his position. "To be loved, this is what I would do. To be loved, this is what I would do."

"I'll be buff and I'll be tan, I will be your macho man. I'll be buff and I'll be tan, I will be your macho man."[7]

In the American culture, as much as women have to battle the "I have to look like Barbie or I'm worthless" mentality, men often feel insecure or not all they should be if they aren't "buff and tan." The result is young men, and older men, who strive for "the look." Why? They may give all kinds of reasons, but if you get them to be honest, a lot of times it's because they want to feel accepted, valued, respected, and secure—loved. They believe being buff and tan will give them the desired results.

There is nothing wrong with having a strong, fit, healthy body. Jesus' occupation as a carpenter probably made him pretty buff and tan. However, men and women respected Jesus not because of his muscles, but because of his character. He loved well.

If our motive behind striving for "the look" is to get love, it needs to be refined by the One who already accepts and values us all no matter what we look like.

The fifth player, a young woman, walked on stage next, turned demurely to the audience, took up the starting stance and said sweetly, "To be loved, this is what I would do. To be loved, this is what I would do."

"I'll be kind and I'll be sweet, I will even kiss your feet. I'll be kind and I'll be sweet, I will even kiss your feet."[8]

This attitude often surfaces when people desperately want the one they love to love them back. They become the proverbial doormat for any morsel of kindness or affection. Women and men with this mentality often become victims of spousal abuse—mental, physical, emotional, and/or financial. These types of relationships typify emotional dependency at its worst.[9]

God's Word admonishes us to be kind and tenderhearted to one another.[10] The problem comes when we become slaves to our need to be loved by individuals to the extent we allow them to manipulate, use, and abuse us. That's not love. That's fear. God has not given a spirit of fear, but power, love, and a sound mind,[11] and living secure in his perfect love drives fear away.[12]

Finally, a young woman entered from stage left and took her starting position. "To be loved, this is what I would do. To be loved, this is what I would do."

"Hug me, kiss me, tell me that you love me. Hug me, kiss me, tell me that you love me."[13]

This person represents the women and men who think the only way to "be loved" is to give themselves to another human. As long as they hug, kiss, or have sex they feel loved. I'm not referring to those who enjoy appropriate touch because touch is their primary "love language."[14] I'm talking about humans who think they can only be valuable, accepted, secure, or comforted in a lover's arms. Sadly, every day all over the world people unwisely give themselves away physically and emotionally in an attempt to feel loved.

People often do foolish things simply to meet love needs. Much grief and damage usually follow these bad choices. However, most folks never consider how deeply these choices and the resulting damage grieve the heart of their creator.

# The Grief Of God

I felt the brisk autumn air embrace me. Thankful for my jacket, I pulled it closer to draw more warmth. The young adult ministry team I led lined up at the door of the Minneapolis nightclub to give the attendant their tickets. Most of the kids in line with us were high school-aged, but sporadically I saw those who appeared to be 20-something.

I thought back to why we'd come. Jeremy, a youth leader from our host church, informed us he had free tickets to a local nightclub. Sunday night the club owners kept the bar closed and didn't allow drinking so they could legally open their doors to teenagers. Jeremy invited us to go with him to the club to hang out with the kids and see if we could get into good conversations.

The attendant asked for my ticket, drawing my mind back to the present. I handed it to him and tried to find my way into the dimly lit club. The music blared as I walked further into the building, and I found myself wishing I'd brought earplugs.

I entered a large, softly lit room with inset house lighting. The two-tiered dance floor already held several young, energetic dancers. A large stage stood at the front of the hall with gigantic video monitors bolted close to the ceiling on either side. The monitors vividly displayed the music video for each song playing.

In an alcove to the left, teens were playing pool on the two tables provided. To my right, a stairway with two flights of stairs led to the second floor where several young people occupied tables and chairs. They sat talking and laughing with friends, and occasionally they glanced down on the dance floor to see who'd arrived. I wondered how they could hear each other over the blaring music.

Strolling around the room and taking in the scenery, I asked the Lord for his heart for the kids and his direction for how to spend my time. A moment later, I decided to go to the second floor and see if I could get into a conversation.

Walking up the first flight of stairs, I casually paused and leaned against the railing to watch the dancers below. My attention immediately went to one young man standing on the second tier of the dance floor. He wore green, glow-in-the-dark knuckles that made quite a visual pattern as he swung his hands furiously and danced wildly to the current number. Amused, I smiled.

Instantly, I heard a quiet voice speak in my mind, "He's the 'see me, notice me' guy, Deonn."

I did a double take. He danced feverishly, but periodically he would look around as if to check to see if anyone noticed him.

"Oh, man," I said sadly as I shook my head slightly.

Turning to my left, I looked up at those seated around the tables on the second floor. Several teens sat in the corner smoking cigarettes and laughing like they were having the best time in the world.

"There's the 'I'll drink, I'll smoke crowd," the voice whispered.

Lowering my head with a heavy heart, I turned to my right. My eyes fell on a slender, nice looking young man with long hair and no shirt strutting up the stairs toward me.

"The 'buff, tan' guy," I whispered, following him up the stairs with my gaze.

At the top of the steps he met a pretty, dark haired young lady, and she wrapped her arms around him snugly. Holding her close, he kissed her head and whispered something in her ear. The "hug me, kiss me" girl's face glowed as she buried her head deeper into his chest.

Suddenly, a wave of grief washed over me like the raging surf of the ocean hitting the rocks. Overwhelmed with deep emotional pain, I fell to my knees with gut wrenching sobs. People walked past me as I sat in a heap on the floor, but I didn't care. I cried, alone with God, sharing his pain over each individual I'd just noticed, but also over those in the generation who were just like them. They desperately wanted to be loved, yet they had no idea they had a generous creator who best knows how to minister to their needs without them getting hurt.

As the sobs grew less intense, I prayed passionately for God to give a revelation of himself to all the ignorant, blind souls damaging themselves and others daily in their frantic quest to feel loved.

The "To Be Loved" drama gets played out in real life every day, and God grieves over the resulting damage to his creation. We need to rewrite the drama for our own lives and inspire others to do the same. To be loved, we need to do what God created us to do—look to him first and foremost to meet our love needs. To do otherwise violates our created design.

## Questions For Reflection or Discussion
1) Which character in the "To Be Loved" skit can you most easily relate to? Why?
2) Most people see God as an angry God ready to punish all sin and stupidity. Few see him as grief-stricken over man's ignorance and rebellion. Why do you think this is true?
3) What struck you most about the nightclub story? Why?
4) Did someone you know, an acquaintance, friend, or family member, come to your mind as you were reading this chapter? If so, pray for them.[15]

*Lord, billions are on a misguided search for love they have not felt. I've been one of them. I've done many unwise things in an attempt to meet my love needs. For any I've not repented for, I repent now. I know I have needs, but I desperately want to learn to look to you to get them met. I want my friends and family to know they can look to you, too. Give me not only head knowledge, but experiential knowledge of these principles I'm learning. I pray I would no longer bring grief to your heart, but much joy as I learn to primarily look to you to be loved. Teach me and empower me to do so. In Jesus' name. Amen.*

# Chapter Five

## *Violating God's Design*

*"...You shall love the Lord your God with all your heart and with all your soul and with all your mind (intellect). This is the great (most important, principal) and first commandment."*
Matthew 22:37-38, Amplified Bible[1]

Imagine yourself a brilliant mechanical engineer in the 1930s. You are gifted and blessed with all kinds of ideas of how to make life easier for the modern housewife. However, your particular interest is to save time and energy for women doing the laundry. Current machines are better than scrubbing boards, but you know you can make it even easier for the ladies. You proceed to diligently study previous designs and search for ways to make the best machine ever.

With delicate care and ingenious precision you design and build the first electric automatic washing machine. You've tested it thoroughly, and it works perfectly. You look at your creation and say, "It is very good."

As the creator of this masterpiece, you understand what needs to be done to ensure it has a long life. Recognizing others won't know how to best care for it if you don't tell them, you put together an instruction manual for anyone purchasing the product. You go into great detail so there will be no misunderstandings. You explain how to plug it in, hook it up to the water source, what settings are required for each load of laundry, etc. You lay the finished instruction manual atop the machine, sigh in satisfaction, and take a walk to think through plans for distribution.

While you are away, your good friend walks uninvited into your house to pay you a visit. Searching every room to find you, he stumbles upon the masterpiece. Dazzled by its beauty, he stares at it in awe. He slowly approaches it, picks up the manual, and reads aloud, "Instructions for using the automatic washing machine."

Suddenly, as if overtaken by some fiend, he declares authoritatively, "This is not a washing machine. This is a refrigerator."

Throwing the instruction manual across the room, he rushes into the kitchen and begins picking up random leftovers, condiments, and a glass jar of pickles. He returns to the masterpiece and puts everything inside. Grinning broadly at his perceived genius, he plugs in the machine and turns on the power.

At that moment you walk into your house and hear the most horrible racket imaginable. Worst of all, it's coming from where you left your creation. Panicked, you run into the room, unplug the machine from the wall, and lift the lid. What you see fills you with horror, amazement, and grief. Broken glass, food remnants, and slimy, greasy liquids clutter the interior of your masterpiece.

Turning slowly to your friend, and with a tear trickling down each side of your face, you say quietly, "I created this to wash clothes. I didn't design it to hold food. Didn't you read the instruction manual?"

He looks at you sheepishly and says, "No. I thought it would make a good refrigerator, and I thought I knew how to work it."

"It's a washing machine, not a refrigerator, and you didn't make it. If you didn't read my instructions for how to use it, what made you think you knew better than I do how it should work?"

"I don't know. I'm sorry. I'll fix it," he says, moving toward the machine.

Brushing tears from your eyes, you reply, "I'm the only one who knows how to fix it because I'm the one who knows everything about it. But you can help. Here is a screwdriver. Do exactly what I tell you."[2]

Perhaps you read this little scenario and thought, "None of my friends are that idiotic." However, if you think about it, humans have been that idiotic since the Garden of Eden. Humanity violates God's created designs daily, and there are consequences for this stupidity. People and things get damaged, and God's good plans for individuals get derailed at worst, or delayed at best.

Every human, except Jesus, has made stupid choices. Scripture declares all others have sinned and come short of God's glory.[3] It recounts story after story of humans who blew it big time. Why does God's instruction manual have these stories? Is it possible he hoped we'd utilize the reasoning abilities he gave us to learn from other people's mistakes and perhaps not make them ourselves?

With this possibility in mind, it would benefit us to ask a couple of questions when trying to learn from stories of Bible characters.

- What possibly motivated this character to make the choice they made?
- What are the consequences (positive or negative) of that choice?

Utilizing this method, I have concluded that most Bible characters who chose badly were trying to get a legitimate love need met in an inappropriate way. They violated their created design and damage resulted. I'll briefly share three examples.

## Samson[4]

As a child, the stories of Samson amazed me. Sunday School teachers presented him as a man raised up by God to judge Israel and to help rescue them from the oppression of the Philistines. They told me he had his great strength because he obeyed God and didn't cut his hair or drink wine. I thought that was pretty cool.

Then Delilah entered Samson's life. The evil witch tricked Samson into telling her the secret of his strength. She had someone cut his hair while he slept, and the Philistines caught him. They poked out his eyes with a hot poker and made him do slave labor. But he got them back in the end. My hero asked God for one more burst of strength in a coliseum filled with Philistines, and he literally brought the house down on top of them. He killed more Philistines that day than in his whole life put together. I thought him brave and courageous, just like every hero should be.

Then I grew up and began to understand the story better. Though God worked through Samson to judge the Philistines, Samson didn't quite live up to hero status in regards to moral character.

- He didn't honor his parents.
- He was arrogant and proud.
- He had a bad temper.
- He had sexual relations with women who weren't married to him.
- He had very bad judgment when it came to the women he loved.

Samson's bad judgment concerning women turned to pure stupidity when it came to Delilah. After being betrayed by his wife earlier in his story, it's astounding he trusted women at all. But Scripture says he loved Delilah. He wanted to trust her. He wanted to believe she loved him and wouldn't do anything to hurt him.

I propose Samson's need to feel loved, and his choice not to look to God to meet the need, clouded his thinking regarding Delilah's motives in wanting to know the secret of his strength. He violated his created design by looking to her to fill his needs for acceptance, security, value, and comfort. His lack of wisdom cost him his sight, his freedom, and eventually his life.

And God cried with grief over his damaged creation.[5]

## King Saul[6]

Most of the time we think of Saul as the evil man who chased David around the hillsides trying to kill him. But Saul wasn't always like that. He started out meek, humble, and obedient to God. In fact, God declared Saul the absolute best choice to be king over his people at the time. God promised to establish Saul's kingdom forever if Saul continued to obey the Lord.[7]

Two of Saul's actions brought about the beginning of the end for him. First, Samuel was late for the appointed offering of the sacrifices to the Lord before the Israelites went into battle. People started getting restless, so Saul performed the priestly act himself. Bad mistake. This action violated several of God's laws. When Samuel arrived, he prophesied Saul's kingdom would not last long.[8]

Second, Samuel told Saul God would be with him to defeat the Amalekites. Samuel commanded Saul to destroy everything, including all the animals, during the battle. But Saul didn't obey. He left the best of the animals and the king alive. Why? Because he feared the people and listened to their voice. Then Samuel made a sad declaration: "You have rejected the word of the Lord, and the Lord has rejected you from being king over Israel."[9]

Saul looked to the people for acceptance, value, security, and comfort instead of God. It cost him greatly. When the people sang the praises of David, Saul's jealousy put him on the path to insanity and attempted murder. He lost the kingdom, but he also lost his mind.[10]

And God cried with grief over his damaged creation.

## King David

Though Scripture proclaims David a man who loved God and sought his heart, there were definitely times he didn't look to God or his ways to minister to his love needs. His most noted failure along these lines, of course, happened in the case of Bathsheba.[11]

As king, David enjoyed many luxuries and privileges. He had a multitude of gifts at his disposal to help minister to his needs for acceptance, value, security, and comfort. But one day when he apparently felt bored, empty, and lonely he saw someone he wanted and decided he'd have her no matter what.

She's married? Who cares—I'm king.

She's pregnant? Oh no! Send for the husband.

He won't sleep with her? Now what? Get him drunk.

Still won't sleep with her? Send him to the front lines so he'll die.

Others died, too? Oh, well. It was for a good cause.

She's free? I'll marry her and no one will be the wiser.

"But the thing that David had done was evil in the sight of the Lord."[12]

Max Lucado in his book *Facing Your Giants* summarized God's feelings declared through Nathan the prophet in 2 Samuel 12:7-9.

> "God's words reflect hurt, not hate; bewilderment, not belittlement. Your flock fills the hills. Why rob? Beauty populates your palace. Why take from someone else? Why would the wealthy steal? David has no excuse."[13]

David's life reflected a man after God's own heart for the most part. But when he started trying to get his legitimate love needs met by going some place other than God first and foremost, he violated his created design. Pain and misery followed.

And God cried with grief over his damaged creation.

All of us have ignored God's instructions and damaged God's creation at one point or another. Our hope lies in the fact our creator is also a redeemer and restorer. As we look to him for answers and do exactly what he tells us, restoration can happen. When we don't look to him, we consistently fall into the traps set for us by the enemy of our souls who leads us into addiction, misery, pain, and death.

The next five chapters highlight some of these traps and explore the miracles of hope and restoration available in a relationship with our creator.

## Questions for Reflection or Discussion

1) Read Matthew 22:34-40. Would it be reasonable to infer from this passage that God created us to relate to him first and foremost? Why or why not?

2) Think of one thing you've done where afterwards you said or thought something like, "I can't believe I was so stupid." As you consider the scenario, do you believe trying to fill a love need motivated your choice to do what you did? What were the consequences of your choice? What do you see as your first mistake in this scenario?

3) What story, phrase, or concept from this chapter stood out to you the most? Why?

*Lord, you declared the most important thing I can do is love you with all of me. I acknowledge you created me in such a way that when I do that, I enjoy abundant life, and I bless those around me. Help me to learn in a deeper way what it means to love you with all of me and to love my neighbor as myself. I don't want to violate my created design any longer. Help me to submit myself to you, and read and apply your instruction manual more diligently. Thank you for what you are teaching me. I love you. Amen.*

## Chapter Six

# *Love Hunger*

*"For the Kingdom of God is not a matter of what we eat or drink, but of living a life of goodness and peace and joy in the Holy Spirit." Romans 14:17, NLT*[4]
*"Thou wilt make known to me the path of life; In Thy presence is fullness of joy; In Thy right hand there are pleasures forever."*
*Psalm 16:11*

The glare of the blazing late afternoon sun blinded me as I drove around the corner toward my house. I quickly lifted my left hand to shield my eyes from the sun's rays and veered back onto the road from the grass where I'd unknowingly strayed.

"Great!" I muttered to myself in annoyance. "Wrecking my car would be all I'd need to make this the perfect horrid day."

Pulling into my driveway, I set the emergency brake and turned off the engine. Draping both arms over the steering wheel, I leaned my head forward and reflected on my day.

The main events scrolled through my mind one at a time. Each of three challenging encounters with coworkers played out. Then I saw myself at the mailbox looking at bills that demanded money I didn't presently have. I lived again the nervous battles in my mind regarding questions on future projects—what, when, where, how?—knowing the answer to all of them was, "I don't know." I felt again the frustrations over computer glitches that hounded me all day. Then I envisioned the grand finale—me walking out of the office saying between clenched teeth, "How am I supposed to do my job if I don't have a working computer?"

Leaning back in my seat, I put my head in my hands and said out loud, "Stop it, Deonn. It's all over. Move on."

I grabbed my briefcase, got out of the car, opened the patio door, and slowly walked into the house. Without giving it much thought, I put my briefcase down, and headed straight for the refrigerator. I surveyed the freezer and the main compartment looking for anything appetizing—anything at all.

Suddenly, I heard a quiet voice in my head say lovingly, "Deonn, what are you doing?"

I stood up straight. Out of nowhere sound bites from my message on love needs drifted through my mind.

"God created us with the need to feel accepted, valued, secured, and comforted. These are legitimate love needs."

"Look to God first to meet your love needs. He's the only one who knows how to best meet them."

"When we look to other people or things to get our love needs met we are violating our created design."

"God grieves when we look to other people or things to meet our love needs because he doesn't enjoy watching us damage ourselves or others."

Slamming the refrigerator door, I walked back to my briefcase, picked it up, and with determination entered my bedroom. Tossing my belongings to the floor, I turned and pushed the power and play buttons on my stereo. When the melody of my favorite worship CD began playing quietly, I laid on my bed, put my arms behind my head, and closed my eyes.

"God," I said, "I had a really hard day. I feel frustrated, insecure, overwhelmed, and a little bit rejected. I recognize I don't need food right now. I know I need love. Please help me."

Immediately my ears became tuned to the words of the song playing.

...My heart is glad that you've called me your own;
There's no place I'd rather be
Than in your arms of love,
In your arms of love,
Holding me still, holding me near,
In your arms of love.²

I began singing with the CD. Within seconds it felt as though 1,000 pounds lifted off my shoulders. My mind started thinking about the wonder of this God who loved me and gave himself for me. Praise and thanksgiving rushed from my heart and out of my mouth for all his awesome blessings. I shed tears of gratitude for his goodness.

Then, a sudden sense of the peaceful presence of God filled my room. I closed my mouth and sat quietly enjoying the stillness. My heart flooded with calming warmth, and I heard a gentle voice speak to my mind, "I'm here, Deonn, and I love you. On good days and on bad days, I love you. I always have and I always will."

I didn't feel hungry any more.

## The Food Problem

Everyone feels emotionally empty once in a while at the end of a bad day—or maybe even in the middle of it. Occasionally, the temptation arises to fill the emptiness or calm the restlessness with food. Why? Because we have a hunger we want satisfied and the normal way to satisfy physical hunger is by eating. Sometimes, however, the hunger we experience stems from emotional causes, not physical ones.

God created us to take in food to nourish our bodies. He also gave us taste buds to aid the enjoyment of our food intake. However, he didn't design us to get our love needs met through food. When we become emotionally hungry and consistently try to fill the hunger with food, a destructive habit pattern may begin to form and lead to serious food addictions, including compulsive overeating.[3]

In their book "Love Hunger," Dr. Frank Minirth and Dr. Paul Meier define compulsive overeaters as "people who are eating to satisfy emotional hungers, hungers of which they may or may not be aware."[4] These authors further assert that compulsive eaters come in all weights. The root of the problem is not how much the compulsive overeater weighs, but why they eat. They become addicted to food as alcoholics become addicted to alcohol.[5] The emotional dependence on food to make people feel good on the inside when everything seems out of control on the outside can be just as deadly as the alcoholic's addiction to alcohol.

Overeaters Anonymous (OA) put together a series of questions to help people determine if they may be a compulsive overeater.

1) Do you eat when you're not hungry?
2) Do you go on eating binges for no apparent reason?
3) Do you have feelings of guilt and remorse after overeating?
4) Do you give too much time and thought to food?
5) Do you look forward with pleasure and anticipation to the time when you can eat alone?
6) Do you plan these secret binges ahead of time?
7) Do you eat sensibly before others and make up for it alone?
8) Is your weight affecting the way you live your life?
9) Have you tried to diet for a week (or longer), only to fall short of your goal?
10) Do you resent others telling you to "use a little willpower" to stop overeating?
11) Despite evidence to the contrary, have you continued to assert that you can diet "on your own" whenever you wish?
12) Do you crave to eat at a definite time, day or night, other than mealtime?
13) Do you eat to escape from worries or trouble?

14) Have you ever been treated for obesity or a food-related condition?
15) Does your eating behavior make you or others unhappy?[6]

If you answered yes to a lot of those questions, you are not alone. In the United States, food addictions have become an epidemic. 10-15% of all Americans suffer from some type of serious eating disorder, and 86% of people with an eating disorder report onset by age 20.[7]

"Experts agree that eating disorders of any type are not really about food. In fact, food is just the 'tool' used to soothe, console, or provide emotional comfort to many who suffer with an overeating condition. It is a way to deal with life when stress, anxiety, or problems arise."[8]

If people don't know or don't believe God can minister to their needs for acceptance, value, security, and comfort when they look to him, they will look somewhere else. A lot of people, many of them Christians, turn to food, and addiction can result.

My friend, Felicia,* grew up in a Christian home. Her parents took her to church, and she loved the Lord from a young age. However, though from the outside this family appeared stable and secure, situations within the family influenced Felicia to feel very insecure. Without consciously doing so, she began to go to food for security and comfort. This habit developed into compulsive overeating with frequent hidden binges.

Felicia secretly struggled for fifteen years, but she is recently finding help and hope in Jesus. The following communicates some of her story in her own words.

> *Insanity is doing the same thing over and over and expecting different results. When it comes to food, I have acted insanely. I have eaten to the point that I am painfully full and chosen to eat even more. I have run to food instead of the Lord to deal with life. I have been so*

*angry at myself that I keep doing the same thing over and over even though I hate what it is doing to my body, my emotions, my spirit, and my relationships. In these times I ask, "Why do I keep going to food when it is causing so much harm in my life?" The answer: Because I am addicted.*

*Sugar has been my drug of choice. I have used it to escape from life, to numb myself, to stuff feelings with food so I don't have to deal with them, etc. I have run to it instead of God for comfort. I have run to it to escape so I don't have to deal with things going on in life— things that God can and will help me face if I run to Him.*

*While struggling with compulsive overeating, there have been times when my response was automatic. I would feel an emotion and impulsively go to food without thinking about it. There have been times when I am eating donuts or candy that I "come to" and suddenly realize what I'm doing.*

*As I have been honest about my addiction and sought the Lord for help, the space of time between wanting the food and the action of eating has increased. This means I now have space to stop and ask God to help me do what I cannot do in and of myself.*

*The biggest turning point for me was when Romans 8:12-13 became real to me. "Therefore, dear brothers and sisters, you have no obligation to do what your flesh urges you to do. For if you live by its dictates, you will die. But if through the power of the Spirit you put to death the deeds of your flesh, you will live" (NLT).[9] I realized by the power of the Spirit, I do not have to fulfill the desires of my flesh.*

*We don't have to live in bondage because God can
break the power of addictions in our lives. He wants to
set us free, but we must cooperate with him and let him
do this work in us.*

Looking to food for comfort rather than nourishment is the
beginning of bondage in this area. However, bad habits in
thought and action can be changed and freedom is possible. A
Christian counselor, a good support system, and a continuing
understanding of God's ability to meet her needs helps Felicia in
overcoming her addiction. Steps toward victory always begin with
acknowledging the problem and asking for help.

I went to the refrigerator that day looking for food because of
hunger—love hunger. When God asked me what I was doing, I
realized I needed emotional nourishment instead of physical
nourishment, and I looked to God to meet the need. Had I not
known and believed God could fill the hunger I felt, I would have
probably eaten more than I should, ended up with a bellyache,
and still felt empty. Instead, I felt peace and a sense of being
overwhelmingly loved by my creator. My hunger disappeared,
and no damage occurred. I call that fine dining.

## Questions for Reflection or Discussion
1) Could you relate to my story about going to the
   refrigerator after a hard day? What would be your comfort
   food of choice? Do you think it's always a negative thing
   to go to food to receive a little comfort? Why or why not?
2) When I looked to God to fill my love hunger, he said, "I'm
   here, Deonn, and I love you. On good days and on bad
   days, I love you. I always have, and I always will." Do you
   believe he feels this way about you, too? Why or why not?
3) What sentence or paragraph in this chapter stood out to
   you the most? Why?
4) Please read this endnote at the back of the book.[10] The
   first step to freedom from addiction is acknowledging the
   problem and asking for assistance. If you struggle with an

eating disorder, tell someone and ask for help. If you don't struggle but know someone who does, pray for him or her right now.

*Lord, I acknowledge the kingdom of God is not about food or drink but about good living, peace, and joy in the Holy Spirit. Your Word declares that in your presence is fullness of joy and you give pleasures forever. I want to live according to kingdom principles, experiencing your joy and the pleasure of your presence in a greater way than ever before. Please continue to teach me how.*

*Father, I confess I have gone to food for comfort instead of nourishment at different times in my life, and I want to learn how to go to you to meet my love needs. Help me recognize temptation and then turn to you instead of food when I feel rejected, insecure, unimportant, and/or in need of comfort. I trust you to assist me as I submit myself to you moment by moment. I love you. Amen.*

# Chapter Seven

## *Emotional Dependency*

*"...the Truth shall set you free, and the Truth has a name...Everything is about him. And freedom is a process that happens inside a relationship with him."*
Papa in The Shack₁

One lone candle burned in my otherwise darkened bedroom. "How appropriate," I thought, looking at the candle and wiping the tears from my eyes. Emotional darkness enveloped me, but a small glimmer of hope in God's ability to come to my rescue flickered. I shuddered involuntarily as I imagined the depth of despair I'd feel without God in my life.

Scooting across the width of my bed and leaning back against the wall, I waited to see if another wave of weeping would wash over me. I'd been mourning my loss for an hour, but it seemed an eternity already. Would the pain ever cease?

"God, I love her so much," I said out loud as fresh tears trickled from my eyes.

"I never asked you not to love her, Deonn," came the whispered reply to my thoughts. "I asked you not to *need* her."

Though the preceding scene appears to describe the emotional pain of having someone close to me die, no one did. The pain I experienced resulted when God in his mercy allowed a severing of an emotionally dependent relationship.

I'm one of many who have experienced the devastating results of emotional dependency. It can develop in same sex or opposite sex friendships, parent-child relationships, and between husbands and wives. Anyone looking primarily to a person to meet his or her love needs for acceptance, security, value, or comfort instead of looking to Jesus can end up emotionally dependent very quickly.

Lori Thorkelson, author of the article *Emotional Dependency – A Threat To Close Friendships,* defines it as "the condition resulting when the ongoing presence and/or nurturing of another is believed necessary for personal security."[2] She explains it could be anything from a platonic relationship that becomes ingrown and possessive to a relationship which develops a powerful, unhealthy, romantic attachment. Either party in the relationship can be emotionally dependent when they demonstrate some or all of the following characteristics.

- Experiencing frequent jealousy, possessiveness, being exclusive, and viewing other people as a threat to the relationship.
- Becoming irrationally angry or depressed when the other person withdraws slightly.
- Losing interest in other relationships except this one.
- Becoming preoccupied with the person's appearance, personality, problems, and interests.
- Being unwilling to make short or long range plans that don't include the other person.
- Being unable to see the other's faults realistically.
- Becoming defensive about the relationship when asked about it.
- Referring frequently to the other person in conversations and feeling free to speak for the other person.
- Exhibiting an intimacy and familiarity with the other person that causes others to feel uncomfortable or embarrassed in their presence.[3]

Steve Prokopchak, Director of Counseling at DOVE Christian Fellowship International, describes some ingredients which may lead to an emotionally dependent lifestyle.

- Insecurity (feeling helpless and hopeless)
- Having a low esteem (not quite measuring up)

- Having a dysfunctional family background (stunting emotional growth)
- Being critical (of self and others)
- Being fearful (fear of rejection, fear of confrontation)
- Practicing self-punishment (playing the martyr's role)
- Having a strong need for intimacy[4]

"These needs and fears create a seedbed for one person's addiction to another person's care for them. Without this dependency, their personal confidence is threatened."[5]

Thorkelson suggests most often when both parties are emotionally dependent, one person appears to be strong and one seems needy. Frequently, though, both are needy. The one appearing strong usually has a deep need to be needed. The one appearing weaker usually controls the relationship. Most of the time neither sees the danger until it has hold of them.[6]

Often in emotionally dependent relationships, individuals look to each other to meet their comfort need. Outside a marriage relationship, this can sometimes lead to inappropriate physical displays of affection, which may eventually lead to sexual acts. Even if sexual actions never occur, a person can improperly give themselves away to the other person emotionally. Sex or no sex, the emotional attachment is out of balance and unhealthy— therefore dangerous.[7]

Emotionally dependent people may look to another person to meet any of their love needs, not just their desire for comfort. But both Thorkelson and Propokchak agree:

> Any relationship will become unhealthy when either party starts looking to a person to meet their needs rather than to God.[8]

Can one person in a relationship be emotionally dependent and the other not be? Yes. However, at some point the relationship will experience strain. The non-dependent will feel pressure to perform a certain way to meet the need of the dependent person. This leads to bondage in trying to meet expectations.

As much as the non-dependent may genuinely love the dependent person, backing away from the relationship, at least for a time, often ends up being the best solution. The dependent person will experience hurt, but God is a God of hope and help. He can minister to the hurting if the one hurt chooses to look to him.[9]

I know this because I lived it. Before my "ah ha" moment with God, I succumbed to emotional dependency four times over the course of many years. One out of four of my emotionally dependent episodes involved a relationship with a friend who wasn't dependent on me.

We were extremely close, but she didn't need me—she loved me. Sitting me down one day, she explained she'd heard the Lord asking her to back away from spending time together. She felt he wanted to change our relationship, but she encouraged me that change didn't have to be bad—just different. Assuring me God wasn't into ripping apart, but building up, she believed the separation would lead to building in both our lives a stronger foundation of healthy relationship in Christ. She promised to let me know if and when the Lord released her to spend time together again, and she walked away.

I felt like somebody died, and I cried for an hour.[10]

From then on, whenever my friend saw me, she'd hug me and let me know she loved me. However, she never called and never made an effort to spend time with me.

Even though I didn't yet understand the love needs concepts presented in this book, I turned to God for help in the midst of my emotional pain. The separation hurt, but when I asked him, he met me in each place of my need for reassurance and love.

Over a year later my friend called to tell me God had spoken to her about our relationship. He'd said one word—restoration. I didn't deserve it, but God gave me the gift again. She's one of my best friends to this day, but I no longer need her—I truly love her.

## The Look Of True Love

So, what does true love look like? Many Scriptures define principles of love, but the most famous love passage is 1 Corinthians 13:4-8.

4 Love endures long and is patient and kind; love never is envious nor boils over with jealousy, is not boastful or vainglorious, does not display itself haughtily.

5 It is not conceited (arrogant and inflated with pride); it is not rude (unmannerly) and does not act unbecomingly. Love (God's love in us) does not insist on its own rights or its own way, for it is not self-seeking; it is not touchy or fretful or resentful; it takes no account of the evil done to it [it pays no attention to a suffered wrong].

6 It does not rejoice at injustice and unrighteousness, but rejoices when right and truth prevail.

7 Love bears up under anything and everything that comes, is ever ready to believe the best of every person, its hopes are fadeless under all circumstances, and it endures everything [without weakening].

8 Love never fails [never fades out or becomes obsolete or comes to an end]... (Amplified)[11]

In Matthew 22 Jesus makes it clear that God's greatest, most important command is to love—to love him, others, and ourselves. In 1 Corinthians 13 it appears this commandment to love requires we make a choice to "act becomingly"—not react based on our pleasant or unpleasant emotions. It implies we might feel jealousy, impatience, or unkindness, but it indicates true love will choose not to act on these feelings. The love God commands is a choice, not an emotion.[12]

Think about it. It would be ridiculous for Jesus to command you to love your enemies[13] if true love required stirring up pleasant emotions. Can you imagine working up warm, mushy feelings for someone who just punched you in the face? Probably not. However, with God's help, you can choose to respond to your enemy in a 1 Corinthians 13 way no matter how you feel in your emotions.

The same holds true when the person isn't an enemy but a friend, boyfriend or girlfriend, parent or child, wife or husband. It doesn't matter how deeply we feel warm mushy emotions toward the person. We must choose to relate with them in a 1 Corinthians 13 way—otherwise we aren't truly walking in love.

With all this in mind, I propose the following to be a pretty good definition of true love.

> True love is not primarily a feeling but a choice we make to honor and act out what God declares to be the highest good for him, others, and ourselves—no matter what.

If this statement reflects reality, and I believe it does, what's the opposite of true love?

1 Corinthians 13:5 states, "...love does not insist on its own rights or its own way, for it is not self-seeking..." It appears the opposite of truly loving someone means being selfish in motive and actions. This, too, is a choice and not an emotion.

In each of my emotionally dependent relationships, I felt deep, warm, mushy feelings I called love. However, I rarely thought through if my motives and actions towards each individual manifested God's highest good for him, the person, and then myself. Most of the time, without realizing it, my dependence on the person to fill my love needs proved my self-centeredness. My emotions felt like love, but my choices displayed the opposite.

I sincerely believe God blessed me with a gift in each of those friendships. Yet, although we included God as a big part of the relationship, in my heart, he slowly faded as supreme love of my life. He attempted to warn me in many different ways of my unhealthy emotional attachments to the gifts he'd given. Yet deception screamed in my mind, "How can love be wrong?" Yielding to the deception, I failed to hear God answer tenderly and sadly, "When it's idolatry and rooted in selfishness, it isn't really love."

Is it wrong to feel love for people or feel loved by them? Of course not. God gives us gifts of relationships to help minister to our love needs. But when we are loving God above all and looking to him first and foremost to get our love needs met, the gifts of relationships he gives us can be enjoyed without damage or bondage.

If we do not choose to operate in what God through Scripture defines as true love, we walk self-centeredly and violate our created design. Damage and emotional grief will eventually follow. However, hope still flickers. If we blow it or have blown it, our creator rescues, redeems, and restores when we let him, and his kindness leads us to repentance. Freedom and healing really do happen inside a relationship with him.

## Questions for Reflection or Discussion

1) What part of the chapter stood out to you the most? Why?

2) "True love is not primarily a feeling but a choice we make to honor and act out what God declares to be the highest good for him, others, and ourselves—no matter what." "It appears the opposite of truly loving someone means being selfish in motive and actions. This, too, is a choice and not an emotion." Comment or journal on each statement separately. Do you agree with each statement? Why or why not? How do any or all of these statements challenge you to think differently concerning love?

3) Do you presently have a relationship with someone you think could be emotionally dependent on either side? If yes, what makes you think so? Talk to the Lord, and others as God directs you, to receive wisdom on what to do to see the relationship become healthy.

*Jesus, thank you for your patience and mercy. Your love amazes me. I acknowledge you are truth, and inside my relationship with you, freedom progressively happens in my life. I want you to be my first love, and I know that I can't really love someone else in the best possible ways without loving you first. I repent for my idolatry in any emotionally dependent relationships I currently have or had in the past. Empower me by your Spirit to honor and to take actions which are the highest good for you, others, and myself. And in all my relationships, please help me point those I love to you above all else instead of drawing their focus to me for my own selfish gains. In your name I pray. Amen.*

# Chapter Eight

## *Sexual Bondage*

*"Or do you not know that your body is a temple of the Holy Spirit who is in you,*
*whom you have from God, and that you are not your own? For you have been*
*bought with a price: therefore glorify God in your body."*
1 Corinthians 6:19-20

It started like all the other classes I'd experienced during my first two weeks in Youth With A Mission's Discipleship Training School. Little did I know God's plan for the day included providing a catalyst to bring much-needed freedom to my life.

We worshipped for a while and then Kip, the teacher for the week, began to teach. He started talking about the ministry of the Holy Spirit. He read from John 16 where Jesus declared that when the Holy Spirit came, he would convict the world of sin.[1]

Kip explained most of us don't like Holy Spirit conviction because it feels uncomfortable. We don't like to feel we've done anything wrong. Often when the Holy Spirit brings conviction, we ignore him and go on our way. Ignore him long enough and we end up with what the Bible calls "a seared conscience" and a "hard heart."[2]

Kip told us conviction is our friend. The Holy Spirit convicts our hearts to inspire us to run to Jesus and repent. It's like fire under our feet to motivate us towards Jesus. It's always specific. We don't just feel guilty for some general sinfulness. When the Holy Spirit convicts of sin, we know specifically what we did that requires repentance.

Condemnation comes from the enemy. It's like fire on top of our head which makes us feel like the scum of the earth. It whispers the lie into our thoughts that Jesus can't love us because we're so wicked, or he'll never forgive us because we're horrible and therefore unforgivable. Condemnation is usually general and is not from God.

The teaching ended by Kip exhorting us to embrace the conviction of the Holy Spirit as part of God's protection for us. If we embrace conviction and respond by running to Jesus and repenting, we are promised forgiveness and restoration of relationship.[3]

Then Kip asked us to bow our heads and close our eyes. He said the Holy Spirit was convicting some of us of sin. If our hearts were pounding really hard as we thought about a particular sin we'd committed or struggled with, he wanted us to stand. Standing represented our commitment to talk with our pastoral care leader. He exhorted us to tell them about the sin so they could help us stay accountable not to sin in that way any more.

My heart pounded like the rapid beat of a bass drum. I felt the gentle nudge of the Holy Spirit urging me to respond to the invitation. With tears in my eyes, I slowly stood. I knew exactly what the Holy Spirit wanted me to confess. Standing took an ounce of courage. The confession would take a ton.

## The Confession
The Prayer Chapel on the YWAM campus measured 15 by 25 feet. No furniture inhabited the structure, but thankfully carpet covered the floor. I rubbed my sweaty palms on my jeans as I sat directly across from Sandra,* my pastoral care leader. Though younger than I, she struck me as someone who loved the Lord and could hear from him. I trusted her, but I still didn't want to have this conversation. What would she think of me?

Looking at me with her blue eyes and tender expression, Sandra said, "So, Deonn, what did God speak to you this week?"

I turned my head and looked out the window. Pointing outside I said, "Can I go over there and tell you?"

She smiled, reached to touch me, and said, "Just go ahead and start talking. It won't be that bad. You'll see."

I waited for a second, looked at her face radiating sincere concern, and then I opened my mouth. The floodgates burst. With tears streaming down my face I told her my secret sin. At 11 years of age I began my struggle with masturbation. Since then, whenever I got upset or depressed, I turned to this addiction for comfort and pleasure.

At about the age of 15, I felt the Holy Spirit's conviction, so I stopped. But the next time things got hard, I did it again. I'd gone as long as two years without falling, and then I'd cave. Shame and guilt over these failures plagued me, but mostly I just didn't want to struggle with it any more.

I glanced at Sandra to see her reaction to this horrible confession. Her eyes reflected understanding and then seemed to sparkle as she calmly said, "Deonn, I struggled with the same thing and God delivered me."

My eyes bugged, my mouth dropped open in shock, and then I let out a sigh of relief. "I always thought I was the only one who struggled with this. No one ever talks about it, so I just figured no one else struggled."

"Lots of Christian men and women struggle with this, Deonn. Because it's done in private and doesn't appear to hurt anyone else, no one wants to talk about it. But many Christians are in bondage to this sin."

"Sometimes I've felt like I wasn't in control of my actions," I said. "It's almost like someone else carried out the act even though I knew it was me. And I always felt so guilty afterwards. I hated it but never seemed to hate it enough not to do it."

"Let me pray for you," Sandra said as she moved closer and placed her hand on my shoulder.

She sat quietly for a minute and then looked at me.

"Deonn, I'm getting a picture in my mind of this big python-like snake wrapped around you from your knees to your neck. Every once in a while it squeezes you, and this look of pain and agony washes over your face. I'm going to pray against this spirit binding you."

"Okay," I replied.

She quietly but firmly began to pray against the lustful stronghold and to command it to leave. She prayed for a while, and then she looked in my eyes.

"Deonn, it's still there," she said sadly.

"I know," I replied with annoyance.

Anger began to rage within me. I started to cry in frustration and addressed the spirit myself. "I hate you!" I cried vehemently. "I belong to God, not you! You are trespassing. I don't want you in my life any more, and you can't be here if I don't want you!"

Immediately, I felt something lift off me starting from the center of my body and moving up past my head. I suddenly felt lighter. I carefully lay back on the ground and heard the Holy Spirit whisper into my mind, "You *are* mine."

"It's gone, Deonn!" Sandra exclaimed.

"I know," I said, crying with joy. My heart overflowed with thanksgiving. It felt great to be free.[4]

## Bondage In The Body[5]

God designed humans with emotional, spiritual, and physical aspects that work together in a wonderful way. He fashioned everyone's body to react to the stimulation of certain body parts by experiencing pleasure. When he looked at the first humans and how he created them to function, he said, "It is very good."[6]

However, his design included the best ways for these "pleasure zones" to be stimulated without damage to his creation. To stimulate them outside of the boundaries he set violates the created design and can lead to sexual bondage.

What are the boundaries set forth in Scripture for stimulating these "pleasure zones?"

- Sexual stimulation should be reserved for a husband and wife relationship only. The marriage bed is undefiled.[7]

You were expecting more? There are no more. That's it. No más. Nada. Zippo. That's all folks.

I can hear it now: "What's wrong with masturbation? It doesn't hurt anybody, and God made me with physical needs that must be satisfied. Lots of respected Christians say it's okay to masturbate."

First, I'd challenge the assertion that masturbation doesn't hurt anybody. It hurt me. Nobody told me masturbating was wrong—nobody would even talk about it. But at age 15 my conscience began to bother me, and I knew it was wrong. Every time I engaged in what some call "do-it-yourself-sex," the seconds of pleasure quickly faded and yielded to hours of remorse and guilt. I actually hated myself sometimes. I'm pretty sure that classifies as damaging.

Secondly, to categorize something as a true need, you'd have to die without it. You need food, water, and protection from the elements (clothing and shelter) to live. You don't need sex. I acknowledge, for males especially, the strength of the sex drive can make it seem like you need relief or you'll die. But you won't.

Thirdly, those respected Christians probably don't see masturbation as harmful because they find no Scripture directly condemning it. There are no Scriptures directly condemning jumping off a cliff either, but does that mean it's wise, loving, or intelligent to do it?

Some may argue masturbation is not a sexual act because no other human is involved. The conclusion of this thinking would be if it isn't intercourse, it isn't sexual. However, the fact the physical sensations and release of bodily fluids when masturbating are similar to what occurs during intercourse makes the assumption that it's not a sexual act totally illogical.

Grantley Morris, founder and primary contributor to the web library NET (www.net-burst.net), states it this way:

> Masturbation, it would seem, is highly addictive for the simple reason that it is sexual, and sex is divinely designed to hurl a husband and wife into a life-long "addiction" to each other. It is clear from Scripture that God created sex for having children and to superglue a man and wife together. It is therefore enticing to conclude that any other use of sex is a perversion of God's plans for sex.
>
> One might also assume that sex was created for expressing marital love and that love focuses on giving, not self-indulgence. If so, to use sex solely to pleasure oneself would seem an abuse of God's gift, like being regularly given money to save up to buy a special gift for someone but, instead, squandering the money on yourself.[8]

God is a generous God who gave mankind a gift to enjoy within the loving boundaries of a committed husband and wife relationship. Engaging in sexual acts outside that boundary will end up hurting somebody because it violates humanity's created design.

"But what if I never get married?" you ask. "What if I never get to enjoy this gift of sex?"

In his book *Sex God*, Rob Bell makes the following conclusion:

> If you are single, and you've been sent messages or it's been hinted at or even said to your face that you are somehow missing something, that you aren't good enough, that you don't fit—that is not true. It's not just that you're fine single. The premise of the Scriptures is that you are able to connect with God and serve God in ways that those who are married can't. The tilt is *for* being single, not away from it.
>
> The last thing Jesus ever says, or even implies, is that people who aren't married are somehow missing out. So according to Jesus, if you aren't having sex, you aren't missing out on anything.[9]

This message contradicts the message of the mass media of our day. Sexual connotations and images are everywhere propagating the demonic gospel that if we aren't having sex, we are missing out on something. It's easy to be sucked into thinking it's true because we're bombarded with the notion continually.

The accessibility of pornography on the Internet also magnifies the temptations to set our minds on sexual things. And if we think about it long enough, we will do it, in some form or fashion. However, Scripture exhorts us to focus our thoughts in a different direction.

- "Set your mind on the things above, not on the things that are on earth...Therefore consider the members of your earthly body as dead to immorality, impurity, passion, evil desire, and greed, which amounts to idolatry." (Colossians 3:2,5)
- "Finally, brethren, whatever is true, whatever is honorable, whatever is right, whatever is pure, whatever is lovely, whatever is of good repute, if there is any excellence and if anything worthy of praise, let your mind dwell on these things." (Philippians 4:8)
- "It is God's will that you should be sanctified: that you should avoid sexual immorality; that each of you should learn to control his own body in a way that is holy and honorable, not in passionate lust like the heathen, who do not know God...For God did not call us to be impure, but to live a holy life. Therefore, he who rejects this instruction does not reject man but God, who gives you his Holy Spirit." (1 Thessalonians 4:3-5,7-8, NIV)[10]

Statistics show that many Christians are in bondage to sexual sin.[11] Addictions to pornography and masturbation are rampant, and sexual intercourse outside a marriage relationship is more common within Christ's body than we'd like to admit. Why? I believe a primary reason is because Christians for the most part don't know how to go to God to get their love needs of acceptance, value, security, and comfort met. And God is grieved.

Without realizing what I was doing, I looked to sex to meet my comfort needs. Addiction/bondage followed. Though technically a virgin, I sexually sinned on numerous occasions. Out of love, the Holy Spirit brought conviction of sin. When I embraced conviction, brought my sin to the light, and desired freedom, God in his love forgave me and set me free. It's a whole lot easier to say no to this temptation now. It still feels good to be free.[12]

No condemnation awaits our honesty of heart; no
punishment. We have only to repent and confess our
sins to have them forgiven and cleansed. We need
merely to love and embrace the truth and we will be
delivered from sin and self-deception.

-Francis Frangipane[13]

## Questions for Reflection or Discussion[14]

1) What stood out the most to you from this chapter? Why?
2) Read and journal your thoughts (or comment if in a
   discussion group) on 1 Corinthians 6:12-20.
3) "The Holy Spirit convicts our hearts to inspire us to run to
   Jesus and repent. It's like fire under our feet to motivate
   us towards Jesus. It's always specific. We don't just feel
   guilty for some general sinfulness. When the Holy Spirit
   convicts of sin, we know specifically what we did that
   requires repentance." Ask the Holy Spirit to bring
   conviction for any place you have gone to sex
   (pornography, masturbation, fantasizing, intercourse
   outside a marriage relationship, etc.) to get your love
   needs met and for self-gratification. Write down what
   comes to your mind, and ask the Lord to forgive you for
   each sin.

*Lord, thank you for coming to dwell within me. I declare that I am
not my own and that I belong to you. I want to glorify you in my
body. I appreciate that you designed me to enjoy sex within a
marriage relationship, and that it is a beautiful gift. I want to
handle this gift with care. I can't change the past, but I can honor
you by utilizing this gift from this day forward only and always as
you designed it to be used. Teach me more and more how to turn to
you when I'm emotionally "hungry, angry, lonely, tired, sick, sad,
stressed, scared, or shameful"[15] so I can allow you to minister to my
need instead of going to sexual outlets for comfort, security, value,
or acceptance. You are good, I need you, and I love you. Amen.*

# Chapter Nine

## *Money Matters*

*"Jesus is not after your money. He is after your heart. How we relate to money is simply indicative of the condition of our hearts."*
Craig Hill and Earl Pitts[1]

Kelly* sat quietly in a pew with the other congregants of the Episcopal Church listening to the rector share the morning address. At one point in the message, he gave a strong exhortation against gambling.

At the mention of the word, Kelly's thoughts drifted to her extended family. Pictures of uncles and cousins who were mafia members and frequent gamblers flashed through her mind. She shook her head sadly as she contemplated the fact their lives, and the lives of their families, were a mess as a result of their lifestyle.

Reflecting further, Kelly thought about the decision she'd made years ago not to gamble. Knowing her family history, she wouldn't even buy a lottery ticket because she didn't want to get sucked into a habit of gambling.

In her thoughts, Kelly said, "Lord, thank you that despite my family background, I don't have a gambling problem."

"Oh, but you do," came the unexpected whisper.

Shocked, Kelly shifted in her seat and thought, "What do you mean, Lord?"

"Every time you use your credit card and don't know if you will have the money to pay it off when the bill comes, you are gambling. You've gambled your way to $17,000 of credit card debt."

Kelly sat in stunned silence as she pondered what she'd just heard. She'd never thought about it that way, but it made sense. She'd known she had accumulated growing financial debt through the years, but until this moment, she'd never considered herself a gambler.

As Kelly evaluated how she'd gotten to this point, the list of reasons for her dilemma seemed endless. However, the root issues underlying those reasons boiled down to a few.

1) Pride, leading to fear of rejection – Being a missionary, she had to raise her own support to accomplish the call of God on her life. Her current support level barely took care of her bills—sometimes. She shunned further fundraising because of fear of what people would think.

2) Low self-esteem/shame (value issues) – Struggles with her weight influenced her to purchase nice clothing to feel better about her appearance. It comforted her to look good even if she'd had to use her credit card to pay for her purchases. Because of her generous nature, she'd give her other clothes away, making her feel better about spending money she didn't have. Giving also gave her a sense of importance in her willingness to bless others.

3) Lack of trust in God as provider (insecurity) – Doubting God's ability to provide for her, Kelly handled things her own way. It was easier to use credit cards than go to God and ask for his direction. Besides, she was afraid of what he'd say—she might not like his answer.

The rector ended his message, and God had gotten Kelly's attention through it. She left the church knowing she needed help.

## Man And Money

I believe the majority of money problems among Christians result from two main issues.

1) Trying to get money and/or utilizing money to meet legitimate love needs in ways contrary to God's design.
2) Not involving God or applying his principles in the process of how money should be acquired or spent.

Notice the love needs mentioned in Kelly's self-evaluation of her money problems.

- She wanted acceptance of friends and family. She didn't fundraise for fear of rejection.
- She looked for value and comfort in the purchase of nice clothing, even when she couldn't afford the purchase in the first place.
- She felt a sense of importance in giving things away but never asked God if he wanted her to give what she gave.
- She struggled for security yet didn't trust God to provide that security. Instead, she trusted in herself and her own ability to figure it out. Credit card debt resulted.

Kelly isn't so different from millions, maybe billions, of people, including Christians, who look to getting money or spending money as the answer to meeting legitimate love needs. Consider the following statements I've heard spoken by Christians.

- "I'm depressed! I think I'll go shopping."
- "Everyone has (fill in the blank). I have to have one, too, or I won't fit in."
- "Tithe? I can't tithe. I barely have enough money to pay my bills."
- "Some day we'll have the money we need to make our dreams come true."
- "Go on a missions trip? But I don't have any money."
- "If only I had more money, I could do all kinds of things for God."

What does each statement imply? At the root of each is a love needs issue and a person thinking or acting on the premise that having money or spending it is the answer to meeting the need.

Money plays a huge part in our day-to-day lives, and it's necessary to accomplish many good things. It's not evil in and of itself. However, Scripture tells us "the *love of money* is a root of all sorts of evil."[2] (Emphasis mine.)

Some Christians make money an idol in their lives and consider having lots of it a major goal to pursue. The love of money instead of the love for God and others takes first place. They look to money for security and utilize money to provide acceptance, to feel important, and/or to buy comfort. All sorts of destructive choices can follow—cheating on taxes, dishonest business practices, accumulating large credit card debt, etc. These actions violate God's principles of love, and the results will eventually be damaging.

God knew money would matter to humans and they would need it to function in the world. He lovingly included plenty of information about money and money management in Scripture. The New Testament alone contains 2,084 verses regarding finances, and 16 of Jesus' 38 parables deal with money.[3]

Outside of God and his principles, there is no wise, loving way to see physical needs met without damage resulting. That's why Jesus exhorted those listening in Matthew 6:33 to "...seek first His kingdom and His righteousness; and all these things shall be added to you."

What does it mean to seek first his kingdom?

God rules and reigns in his kingdom as supreme authority. That's what the king of a kingdom does. To seek his kingdom first implies yielding to his kingly authority and doing what he says above what anyone else says.

Fortunately, God is a generous ruler who loves us unconditionally and seeks our highest good always. To do what he says is always the most loving thing, and obedience to him is always logical, reasonable, and intelligent—even if we don't completely understand the reasons why he's asking us to do something.[4]

What does it mean to seek first his righteousness?

The Greek word translated righteousness means "the act of doing what is in agreement with God's standards" or "the state of being in proper relationship with God."[5]

If we seek God's desires and follow his principles for how to utilize the finances he's put into our hands, and we do so with a loving motivation to please him, he will guide us, and our needs will be met. It's his promise.

God wants to be involved in every part of our life—not so he can control us, but so he can help us and others. He knows everything, sees everything, and knows what's best for everyone. He's God, and we're not. Why wouldn't we ask him how we should best use the finances he puts into our hands? Why wouldn't we obey him when he asks us to give away something he gave to us in the first place?

My youngest sister informed me one day that she and her husband were sending me a check in the mail. She didn't tell me how much they'd sent, but said it should arrive soon. When I hung up the phone, the Holy Spirit whispered to my mind that I needed to send the money to a friend of mine. I simply said a quiet yes in my heart and went on my way.

A few days later, I received the check for $525. Whoa! I didn't expect it to be that much. I wavered momentarily in my decision, but then realized in God's eyes the money didn't belong to me. To keep it would be stealing. I wrote a check for $525 and sent it to my friend. She thanked me profusely because the gift was so timely.

In my time of need, I've been on the receiving end, too. One day I got a check for $3,000 from a good friend who felt from the Lord to send it to me. She had no idea the head gasket on my car blew out ($1,500 repair) and my taxes were due soon. She simply obeyed God's direction, and through her, he met my need.

If we belong to God, so does everything we "own." We are meant to be stewards of finances and possessions. If God is our master and we trust his love for us, we will trust him to provide for our needs and obey him when he asks us to give something away.

However, if we put our trust in money and in our own wisdom of how to acquire it or manage it, at some point we will become a slave to worry and fear in financial matters. It will also hinder God's good desire to bless us and others through us.

If all God's kids intentionally allowed him to direct them on how to acquire and spend finances, I believe no true follower of Christ would be in want of clothing, food/water, or shelter. Unfortunately, not all of God's kids are seeking his kingdom and his righteousness first in the area of finances. The result? People suffer, and God grieves.

God has something to say about the way we acquire and spend money. Are we seeking his kingdom first in the realm of finances if we don't ask him what to do with money we receive? Do we love him with all our heart, mind, soul, and strength if we don't involve him in the area of finances?

God wants to free us from all bondages—including financial ones. But the first step to freedom is always the same—we have to realize and admit we need help. Then we must cry out to God in repentance for fear, pride, selfishness, and unbelief, and ask him to show us what to do. In his generosity and love, he will guide and make a way where there seems to be no way.

## The End Of The Story

When Kelly acknowledged she needed help to get out of her financial mess, she went to a financial counselor. She considered filing for bankruptcy, but the counselor encouraged her not to. He suggested strict accountability and a payment plan strategy to deal with her debt.

After some serious repentance and prayer asking for God's help, Kelly made herself accountable to two mature Christian friends. They drafted a contract that stated:

- Exactly how much extra Kelly would pay on the credit cards each month.
- Kelly would make herself accountable for every single penny she spent.
- A credit card requiring monthly payoff would be the only card used until the accountability partners agreed to the contrary.

With this plan, the debt would be cleared in five to ten years. Kelly signed the contract and began to operate accordingly. Though challenging, every time temptations arose to spend money in ways contrary to the contract, she'd remember the mess she'd made of things before. She decided to look to God to minister to her love needs and her physical needs, and trust him with the results.

Amazingly, the whole debt ended up being wiped out in three years. Kelly realized when she was faithful to humble herself to honor God by seeking first his kingdom and his righteousness, he faithfully helped her gain financial freedom. He proved his Word true once more. Nothing is impossible with God.[6]

## Questions for Reflection or Discussion

1) "I believe the majority of money problems among Christians results from two main issues. One, trying to get money and/or utilizing money to meet legitimate love

needs in ways contrary to God's design. Two, not involving God or applying his principles in the process of how money should be acquired or spent." Do you agree with these statements? Why or why not?

2) "God wants to be involved in every part of our life—not so he can control us, but so he can help us and others. He knows everything, sees everything, and knows what's best for everyone. He's God, and we're not. Why wouldn't we ask him how we should best use the finances he puts into our hands? Why wouldn't we obey him when he asks us to give away something he gave to us in the first place?" What could be the possible answers to the questions in this paragraph? What are some Scriptures that address those possible answers?

3) What other sentence or concept from this chapter stood out the most to you? Why?

*Lord, I acknowledge your concern for me regarding finances is not about my money but about my heart. You love me and don't want me hurt. You knew I'd have issues regarding money and lovingly gave me principles in your Word to help me. I acknowledge I am not wise enough or loving enough to know the absolute best way to deal with financial issues. Please help me learn to look to you for guidance in financial matters and to look to you instead of money to meet my love needs. I want to learn to seek first your kingdom and your righteousness. Thank you for loving me so much. Amen.*

# Chapter Ten

## *When Fun Isn't Funny*

*"Do not love the world, nor the things in the world...For all that is in the world, the lust of the flesh and the lust of the eyes and the boastful pride of life, is not from the Father, but is from the world."*
1 John 2:15-16

Charged with tension so thick David* imagined he could cut it with a knife, the atmosphere in his home today seemed anything but homey. The normally quiet, peaceful family room felt like a courtroom—and he was the defendant.

David's mom and dad sat on the couch, and David sat in the recliner. Jimmy,* David's brother, stood in the kitchen. The kitchen opened into the family room, and Jimmy made it obvious he was listening to every word.

"Son," David's dad began, "Jimmy saw the online post you made to your friends about leaving to do this program for five months. But you told them you'd be back after that. Are you serious about getting free of this addiction or not? If you are, you can't go back to them."

"But they are my friends, Dad. I can't just cut them out of my life."

"They are part of the problem that is destroying your life, David," his mom said sadly. "They can't help you because they have the same addiction."

His dad looked David in the eyes and said calmly, "You have a choice, Son. You can do this program knowing we will do everything we can to help you get close to the Lord and see you free of this addiction. Or," he pointed to the front door, "you can choose to walk out that door today, live as you please, and be responsible for yourself without our help. We'll always love you, but enough is enough."

Sadness gripped David's heart. The pain in his parents' eyes tore at his soul.

"Maybe I should leave. Maybe that would be best for everyone."

Like a racehorse out of the stall at the sound of the gun, Jimmy bolted out of the kitchen toward David. He grabbed David's shirt with his left hand and pointed his right forefinger in David's face.

"Dave, do not mess this up!" Jimmy yelled. "Do not mess this up! If you continue doing this stuff and choose to walk out that door, you'll end up killing yourself and lying dead somewhere in the street within the year!"

As if suddenly realizing the violence of his actions, he released David's shirt and stood back. His face shone red with anger and frustration as he continued yelling and pointing his finger in David's face.

"You are pretty much wrecking your life, dude. You're wrecking our family, too. All the choices you're making are screwing everything up. If you walk out that door, you will end up dead!"

David felt liked he'd been slapped in the face by Jimmy's words. The jolt seemed to knock some sort of invisible scales off his eyes. He suddenly saw things clearly for the first time in a long time.

What was he doing to his family? What was he doing to himself? Jimmy was right. If he left and didn't do this program, he probably would end up dead in the next year. In that moment, for the first time in three-and-a-half years of addictive behavior, he realized he had a problem, and he needed help.

He looked at Jimmy, whose face clearly revealed his frustration and anxiety. Then he looked at his parents, who had the same look of anxiety but whose eyes radiated love David felt he didn't deserve.

"You're right, Jimmy," David said. "I need help." He looked at his parents. "Mom, Dad, I'll do the program and do my best to seek God in the process. I don't want to live like this any more."

## David's Problem

As much as it sounds like David's addiction could have been to alcohol or drugs, he was actually addicted to video games. Though most would say that too much "gaming" seems harmless compared to the dangers of a drug overdose, David's story shows it can be destructive nonetheless.

Being held back in first grade influenced David to fear failure, which led to the development of a performance mentality. That didn't present too many problems until he entered college. While there, the pressure to succeed overwhelmed him, and he became involved in role playing games on the computer to escape reality. Not pleased with who he was in real life, David began to sink more and more of his time and thoughts into the character he was playing in the game. The acceptance and respect he felt in his "guild"[1] covered up the pain and shame of all his perceived failures in life. Soon his game world seemed more secure, safe, and welcoming than the real world.

Before long, David had concocted elaborate lies in an attempt to hide his game life. The lies reached a pinnacle when he flunked out the first semester of his sophomore year in college because he never went to class.

His parents received his grades, and his dad confronted him about them. He told his dad the college made a mistake. He swore those grades weren't his and that the records department messed up. Wanting to believe him, his dad went to the computer to write the college and let them know of the mistake. David then told the truth for fear of embarrassing his father.

For the next two years David lived at home, worked, and took classes at a junior college. His parents forbade him to play those games or to use their computer at home without supervision. But David had to have his game world with his guild friends, and nothing else mattered. He acquired parts and built his own computer, which he kept hidden from his family.

The downward spiral continued as he began racking up phone charges by calling the guild members to converse in real life. Everything was great until his parents got the phone bill for the calls.

Heartbroken and upset by yet another of their son's deceptions, his parents attempted to help him by having concerned, caring Christian friends talk with David about his problem. But he'd learned how to play the Christian game, too. He said what he knew people wanted to hear, but nothing changed in his heart. His addiction continued until the day his brother almost literally slapped him in the face.

## The Entertainment Trap

Video games are only one of many forms of entertainment that can become a snare to humanity when taken to extremes. Television, movies, theater, dance, books, sports, music, games, hobbies, and social networking avenues can capture our imaginations to such an extent they become addictive. People from many cultures have become so entertainment driven that much of their time and resources are gobbled up in pursuit of the next entertaining thing.

Why is entertainment so alluring? Consider some of the reasons people would typically give if asked why they pursue a form of entertainment. Depending on the day and the circumstances, the same person could answer the question with any, or many, of the following:

- I'm tired, and this relaxes me.
- I'm bored, and it's something to do.
- It's good exercise, and I enjoy it.
- It's good stress relief.
- It's a social outlet for me. I enjoy the relationships.
- I like to learn, and this is educational.
- It's an outlet for me to express myself creatively.
- It's an escape from the pressures of life. It provides a diversion from the challenges of reality.
- It's fun.

Relief, cheer, support, or pleasure is the root of each reason given. It would appear we like to be entertained because it ministers to our comfort love need.

You may be thinking, "Okay, we like to be entertained because it fills a love need. Is that wrong?"

I find no Scripture to back the notion God is opposed to us enjoying entertainment in the general sense. Dancing, dramatic performances, story telling, fishing, running races, and many more entertaining activities are mentioned in the Bible with no hint of condemnation.[2]

However, Scripture strongly supports the truth that God is opposed to his creation being damaged. And damage occurs when people operate contrary to the law of love.

Remember the definition of love? True love is not primarily a feeling but a choice we make to honor and act out what God declares to be the highest good for him, others, and ourselves— no matter what. The opposite is selfishness.

If by engaging in our preferred forms of entertainment we disobey God's commandment to love him with all our heart, mind, soul, strength and love our neighbors as ourselves, we violate our created design. If we violate our design, damage will eventually result.

How do we know if we are in danger of damaging ourselves through entertainment?

- If the modes of entertainment we enjoy influence us to dwell in our thinking on things Scripture exhorts us away from (i.e. sexual sin, fear, unwholesome/silly talk, etc.),[3] we are on the road to damage.
- If we begin to care more about our preferred forms of entertainment than spending time with God or others, we are on the road to damage.
- If we become obsessed with entertainment to the point it interferes with our schoolwork, job, or other responsibilities, we are on the road to damage.
- If we put more money into our forms of entertainment than we do into supporting God's work, or we put ourselves in debt through our pursuit of entertainment, we are on the road to damage.
- If we feel the need to hide the fact from friends and loved ones that we are involved in certain forms of entertainment, we are on the road to damage.
- If we look primarily to our forms of entertainment to fill our love needs instead of God, we are on the road to damage.

As children of God, the Holy Spirit dwells within us to guide us and lead us in the way we should go. He'll nudge our hearts with conviction if we are going down an unhealthy road regarding entertainment. We must listen and obey to stay safe.

Sometimes, though, when we're "hard of hearing" because we've been blinded by the lies of the enemy, God uses other people to speak words of wisdom into our lives. They may see the potential dangers of the road we're traveling with our entertainment, and we may not. If we love God and want his best in our lives, we will listen to what others have said and take it to the Lord to ask him if what they've seen is true. Even if we think they're wrong, we should ask God to show us if they are right because *anyone* can have blind spots.[4]

God can minister to every love need in the best possible ways without damage. He wants to be involved in every part of our lives, including the entertainment part. As we submit our entertainment choices to him who knows us best, we'll find ourselves not lacking fun—just lacking damage.

In case you're curious, David did attend that five-month program. He also completed a second phase of training and served in missions full-time for several years. He's not perfect, but he has experienced freedom from his addiction as he's made choices to look to God instead of video games to minister to his love needs. Believe it or not, his adventures with God in the real world have taken him to a much higher level of challenge, power, and joy than any video game ever could.

## Questions for Reflection or Discussion

1) What stood out the most to you in this chapter? Why?
2) Read the quote at the beginning of this chapter from 1 John 2:15-16. What do you think these words mean as they relate to the topic of entertainment?
3) Look again at the list of danger signs of entertainment that can lead down the road to being damaged. Which one or ones stand out to you? Why?

*Lord, I don't want to love the world or the things of the world more than I love you. I don't want anything to divert me from my relationship with you or to propel me down the road to damage. I give the Holy Spirit permission to convict me if I involve myself with any sort of entertainment that will grieve you, harm others, or harm me. Leaning into the Holy Spirit for his help and power, I will choose to respond to his conviction and avoid the dangerous paths possible through entertainment. I will look to you first and foremost to get my comfort needs met and acknowledge my need for your help in it. I love you. Thank you for what you are teaching me. Amen.*

# Chapter Eleven

## *Why Is It So Hard To Believe?*

*"For Thou, Lord, art good, and ready to forgive, and abundant in loving kindness
to all who call upon Thee." Psalm 86:5
"Call to Me, and I will answer you, and I will tell you great and mighty things,
which you do not know."
Jeremiah 33:3*

Perhaps you've read everything written to this point, had some "ah ha" moments along the way, and can understand everything I've said intellectually. But maybe there is a nagging question tugging at the corner of your thinking as to whether it's all *really* true.

Perhaps you question some of the premises of this book because you've not experienced God the way others mentioned and I have. You wonder how the creator of the universe, whom you can't physically see or touch, can minister to every love need when you aren't sure he ever has before? Can he, or will he, really do it? And this relationship/friendship with God stuff—can that really happen?

Why is it so hard to believe? I'd like to suggest some of this might be hard to believe because of our misconceptions of God and his character.

### Misconceptions Of God

Before teaching on love needs in a YWAM School of Evangelism several years ago, I felt the Lord impressing me to do something different. He told me to ask the students what God had revealed to be their biggest misconception about him and his character. Secondly, he told me to ask what they felt influenced them to have the misconception in the first place.

I wondered what these questions had to do with getting love needs met from God, but I obeyed. After everyone shared, the connection became apparent.

First, let's look at what they believed influenced them to have the misconceptions. Each answer fell under one of the following categories:

1) Parents who modeled truth poorly, or not at all, because of their own misconceptions, emotional issues, and/or lack of knowledge.
2) Poor teaching at church (legalistic, inaccurate, or incomplete) because church leaders had misconceptions, issues, and/or lack of knowledge.
3) Seeing the hypocrisy of Christians in the church, which influenced distrust and disbelief in God.
4) Bad experiences in life which tended to foster negative concepts about God.
5) Their own choices (i.e. making wrong assumptions, lack of trust, or rebellion).

The misconceptions revealed during their training fell under one of the following:

1) Everything that happens is God's will.
2) God doesn't speak today except through the Bible.
3) God is far away and too busy running the universe to personally care about me as an individual.
4) I've done too many bad things for God to love me or forgive me.
5) God is a legalist who only cares that I perform the rules dutifully. He isn't relational.
6) God will abandon me some day.
7) God won't take care of me, (i.e. he won't provide or protect).

These inaccurate concepts had the students questioning God's love, faithfulness, generosity, kindness, desire or ability to have a personal relationship with them, and his desire to forgive. When carefully considered, each of their misconceptions boiled down to saying simply, "God is not good or relational."

I then saw how the survey connected to love needs. To be in a position to want to go to God to minister to our love needs instead of other people or things, we need to trust he is good and that he can, wants to, and will relate with us.

If we wrongly believe God is not good or relational, we won't allow him to get close. We'll build walls against him to protect ourselves even while we do all the religious duties required by church systems which supposedly prove our allegiance to him. It's also possible we'll do all the religious duties simply to appease God so he won't send us to hell. Or, maybe we'll do them just so we can be a part of the social life at the church and fit in. None of this constitutes right relationship with God.[1]

For the sake of our love needs discussion, it is vital to address these two misconceptions: Everything that happens is God's will, and God is not relational. If we have these misconceptions, we will not look to God with an open heart to minister to our love needs.

## The Will Of God *Is Not* Always Happening

A few years ago I went to Kenya to teach forty Christian college students some foundations for biblical Christianity. As I got to know the students, I learned Sylvia's* parents were killed in an automobile accident, leaving her an orphan. A few years later she experienced a horrifying rape. Well-meaning Christians, who believed everything that happens is the will of God, tried to help and encourage her by letting her know everything transpires for a reason. They assured her God's purposes were unclear in these tragic situations, but it would all be for her greater good at some point. She would just have to accept it.

Their "comforting words" didn't help much, but because Sylvia wanted to go to heaven and see her parents again some day, she went to church and fulfilled all the religious duties required of her. However, there was no light in her eyes or joy in her expressions. When I met her, I sincerely wondered whether she actually knew God relationally at all. I prayed God would minister to her in a special way through the week.

During one of my first teachings, I presented as a misconception the notion that everything that happens is the will of God. We looked at 2 Peter 3:9 which says "...God is not willing for any to perish but for all to come to repentance."[2]

I asked the students if, from what they observed, all people repented. They said no. I concluded, if everyone doesn't repent, it seemed logical the will of God wasn't always happening.

Since I'm convinced it's dangerous to make a doctrine based on one verse, I had them then turn to Matthew 6:9-10 where Jesus taught the disciples how to pray. Jesus said, "Pray then in this way: 'Our Father who art in heaven, hallowed be Thy name. Thy kingdom come. Thy will be done, on earth as it is in heaven.'"

I reasoned with them by asking the following questions:

- Why would Jesus tell the disciples to pray God's will would be done on earth if everything that happens is the will of God already?
- If everything that happens is going to be God's will anyway, what is the point of praying and interceding for people at all? Yet Scripture exhorts us in many places to intercede for our leaders, pray without ceasing, pray for our enemies, etc.[3]
- Is God arbitrary and wants us to pray just because he said so? Does he think we need to pray because it produces character in us even though it doesn't really affect anything else? Or, do our prayers really

affect the heavenlies in such a way they can
somehow facilitate God's will being done on the
earth?

I proposed God isn't arbitrary and he doesn't tell us to pray his
will be done on earth simply to build character in us. He tells us
to pray because it makes a difference. He wants and needs men
and women to pray his will to come on the earth.[4]

If God's will isn't always done, I suggested there must be other
influences[5] besides God affecting our world significantly. I asked
the students to consider the following list of five influences which
Scripture implies work in the spiritual and physical realities of
our existence.

1) God
2) Good and bad angels (Satan and his demons are in this
   category.)
3) Other people's choices – good or bad
4) Our own choices – good or bad
5) Circumstances (Often people are involved in these
   circumstances but no wicked hearts are at work. Some
   would call these accidents.)[6]

I showed the students where Scripture clearly teaches Satan and
demons exist. The devil consistently attempts to influence
humans away from God and his perfect love through tempting us
to act selfishly (Luke 4). He hates God and he hates humanity
because God loves us. He will tempt us and fight against us until
the day we die. However, God doesn't will people to be
demonized or destroyed by demonic influences. Otherwise, Jesus
would neither have cast demons out of people nor provided
Scriptures to show us how to battle against them.[7]

Then I turned our attention to the fact God does not will for
others to hurt us. It's not his idea for people to abuse their
children, murder their spouses, or rob a bank. People choose to
be selfish. Selfish choices are destructive because God designed us

to walk in love to function best. The Creator's choice would always be for humans to walk in love toward one another.[8]

Next, I asked them to consider how each of our own choices has consequences that influence our lives. God doesn't will that any of us sin and damage ourselves, other people, and creation. He grieves over it. If we sin, he is willing to forgive and restore, but he desires that sin never occur.

Finally, I addressed the concept of "stuff happens." We live in a sin-cursed world and often many horrible things occur because of the wicked intent of man's heart. However, some events take place with no wicked heart motive involved. People die in one-car automobile accidents. Motorcycles fall on two-year-olds. A brother runs over his little sister because he doesn't see her. A door is flung open and someone's nose gets broken. No human means for these painful circumstances to happen, but they happen.

The question then becomes, "Does God will these things?" Humans usually look for someone to blame for situations which cause pain. If man can't be blamed, usually the finger gets pointed at God. However, sometimes stuff just happens. No one has a wicked heart in the scenario, and it's not the will of God. Accidents are called accidents because nobody intended for them to occur.

With this foundation and the other teachings presented that week on the character of God, Sylvia gained a new perspective. Instead of having to convince herself her parents died in a car wreck and left her an orphan because God willed it for her greater good, she could see it as a tragic accident. Instead of thinking God wanted her raped to work some greater good in her life, she saw it as an evil choice by a selfish man who needed Jesus in his life. With this understanding, she could run to God and ask him to minister his comfort and his healing in the midst of her pain instead of blaming him for the pain. She decided she wanted to experientially know God because she could actually believe he was good.

God really is good, and his will isn't always being done. He doesn't will for anyone to perish but for all to come to repentance. He doesn't choose some for heaven and some for hell. People make their own choices, often influenced by the enemy of their souls. God wants everyone, all, and whomsoever will to come into intimate relationship with him.[9]

## God *Is* Relational

I've spent a good deal of time in this book building a scriptural foundation supporting the position that God created and designed each human to be in a close relationship with him first and foremost. Let's assume we agree with this premise. The next question posed by seekers and skeptics alike is how does God relationally connect with those he created for relationship with himself? Humans can't see him or touch him. How do we relate with someone we can't see or touch?

Perhaps it would help to first look at how humans relationally connect. If we think about it, our primary means of building and retaining a healthy relational connection is verbal and non-verbal communication. This could include written or spoken words, a look, a touch, a gift, an act of service, being physically present with someone by choice, and the list goes on. Misunderstandings sometimes occur, but there could be no healthy, vibrant human relationships without communication.

If God made us in his image, it seems logical that a healthy relationship with him would be built through verbal and non-verbal communication, as well. Consider:

1)  The Holy Spirit inspired humans to write about God's interaction with humanity so we could learn about him and how to live according to our created design. From

Genesis to Revelation we read about how God spoke to people in a myriad of ways. God does speak.[10]

2) He longs for individuals to spend time with him.[11] He enjoys our company.

3) He particularly watches over those of us who want relationship with him and longs to show himself strong on our behalf. His eye is upon us because he cares for us.[12]

4) He made his reality known in a physical way over and over again in Scripture. Some in Scripture experienced his reality through dreams or visions. Others experienced him when he displayed his power to heal. Also, a lot of believers in the here and now talk of "feeling" his presence or his touch. We can physically experience him.[13]

5) In chapter three I wrote about the giving God. He didn't stop with the gift of his son. He continues to give gifts to his children all the time.

6) Jesus said he came to serve, not to be served. The greatest in the kingdom is the servant of all. Think about Jesus' continued acts of service to us through being our intercessor and high priest.[14] These acts of service are non-verbal communications of His love toward us.

From these examples we can conclude we honor, love, and serve a relational, personal God. He can and does communicate with us verbally and non-verbally. It's just a matter of believing this truth and "listening" and "looking" for how he may be communicating his love today.

He is God, the creator of all, and he loves us. It's time to exchange the lies we've believed about him for the truth of what he's really like.[15] He's good, and we can trust him. He's relational, and we can experientially know him. We need to recognize our misconceptions of God so barriers are removed to building the healthy relationship with him he desires and deserves. Then we will be more willing to look to him to minister to the love needs we so long to have met.

# Questions for Reflection or Discussion

1) Look again at the list of the SOE students' misconceptions of God. Which one/ones have you believed in the past? What helped you recognize the lie/lies? Which one/ones do you realize you still believe? What influences you to believe it/them?

2) What word, phrase, or concept stood out the most to you in the section titled "The Will Of God *Is Not* Always Happening?" Why?

3) Dr. Gary Chapman in his book "The Five Love Languages" states that most people have a "love language" which best communicates love for them. The five he writes about are Words of Affirmation, Quality Time, Physical Touch, Gifts, and Acts of Service.[16] How do those "languages" compare to point 1 and points 3-6 about how God communicates verbally and non-verbally listed under the last section in this chapter titled "God *Is* Relational"? What conclusions do you draw from these comparisons? Why?

*Father, I declare with the Psalmist, "For Thou, Oh Lord, art good." I thank you this is the truth. I pray you will bring to light any doctrine, philosophy, or theology I believe that would deny that truth if I took it to its logical conclusion. Help me use my "powerful God-tools for smashing warped philosophies, tearing down barriers erected against the truth of God..."[7] I want nothing standing in the way of intimate friendship with you.*

*I call to you now, Lord, believing you to answer me because your Word says you want to show me great and mighty things which I do not know. You are a God who speaks, and I'm grateful. Please continue to show me all you want me to know so I can trust you more, love you in deeper ways, and look to you instead of other people or things when my "love tank" is dry. I declare again, "You are good!" It's true!*

# Chapter Twelve

## *Try It—You'll Like It*

*"...He is everything that is perfect and excellent and complete and flawless; everything we will ever need Him to be to fulfill us..."*
*Joy Dawson*[1]

Let's summarize what we've learned so far.

- God created man with a need to feel accepted, valued, secure, and comforted. These are our basic love needs. They are good, not bad.
- God designed us primarily for loving friendship with him and then relationships with others. He is our most comprehensive relationship, and we should look to him above all other things to get our love needs met because he knows best how to meet them.
- Our giving God wants to bless us with good gifts to help minister to our love needs. But if we take our eyes off the giver and focus on the gift, damage will eventually happen.
- God designed us to function best spiritually, mentally, emotionally, and physically when we love him first. To love other people or things first is idolatry. Idolatry violates our created design. Violate the created design, damage will occur.
- We grieve God's heart when we look to other people or things to get our love needs met because of the resulting pain to us and others.
- Going to food, relationships, sexual sins, money, or entertainment to minister to love needs instead of looking to God can lead to bondage/addiction. Anyone in bondage/addiction can know and apply the truth of God's Word in a relationship with Jesus and be set free.[2]

- Our misconceptions of God hinder our willingness to trust him to minister to our love needs. Misconceptions about him and his character must be recognized and dealt with. Exchanging the lies about God for the truth revealed through his communication with mankind is essential to trusting him.

Understanding these concepts intellectually is a good thing. However, change never occurs through intellectual assent alone. Truth isn't truth learned until it's been applied to our lives.

## Truth Applied

"You guys don't understand!" Mandy* exclaimed as she sat on the sofa across from me, her eyes wet with tears.

She had that right. I stared at her in amazement, unsure of what had prompted the emotion, but very curious to find out.

The two of us sat with six other women in the dorm lobby. I'd arranged this Christmas celebration for our last small group meeting at the end of Mandy's School of Evangelism lecture phase. Up to this point, the evening had been filled with food, fun, laughter, and joy in bestowing gifts on one another. Now we all sat looking at Mandy, and I wondered what she would say next.

"What's wrong?" one of the girls asked.

Still wiping tears from her eyes, Mandy launched into her story.

Several weeks earlier, Mandy had been out for a walk to spend time with the Lord. She found herself thinking about the teaching I'd given on looking to God to get all our love needs met. She'd been unsure of the truth of my words but decided to see if God really could or would meet her current felt need.

"God," she'd prayed, "Deonn says you can meet all our love needs if we will look to you to get them met instead of other people or things. If what she said is true, I need a little romance in my life. I know it might seem silly, but can you give me a flower, a poem, and a song?"

She'd waited for a response, but after a minute or two of silence, she'd decided maybe God did think her a little silly. She'd continued her walk and began thinking about other things.

A few days later, Mandy opened her car door to find a single red carnation laying in the driver's seat. A card sat beside it. In block letters the card simply stated, "May your day be blessed with all things beautiful. Love, Jesus."

Shocked, she'd stood looking from the flower to the card. She'd inhaled the scent of the carnation and smiled. Jesus had given her a flower. Though her logical mind knew some person put it there and signed the card "Jesus," she'd prayed for a flower and gotten one. It seemed to be part one of the answer to her prayer.

During her time with the Lord a couple of days later, Mandy had written in her journal some thoughts concerning her father. Much hurt remained regarding relationship situations with her dad, and Mandy journaled some of her feelings.

As she'd written, words began coming to her mind that didn't seem to be her own. She'd quickly written them as they came. When no more words flowed, she'd put down her pen and picked up her journal to read what she'd written. The realization suddenly dawned that she'd written a poem—a poem of love from God.

Astounded, she'd read the poem again. Could this be part two of the answer to her prayer? She'd been given a flower and a poem of love. Would he really be able to give her a song, too?

Mandy had put down her journal and prayed out loud, "Okay, God. You've given me a flower and a poem. I'm grateful. Thank you. If you give me a song, though, I don't want it to be just any old love song on the radio. Please let me know it's really from you. I'd like it to have my name in it."

Mandy stopped telling the story at this point and looked at me with sincere gratitude beaming from her eyes as she dried the remaining tears. Now I understood.

I'd drawn Mandy's name for our small group gift exchange. I'd just given her the gift God told me to give her when she'd burst into tears. I looked down at my guitar. Then I looked at the words to the chorus of the song God had inspired me to give Mandy as her Christmas gift.

> Mandy, my love for you is great, it knows no limit.
> It's freely given, won't you freely receive?
> You're precious, you're unique, my love,
> No one can take your place.
> So understand I love you like no other,
> For there is no other like you.

## He Can Meet The Love Need

I've told this story many times in teaching settings. Most young women dreamily say, "Ahhhhh" and look like they want to cry. Most guys, unless they are romantics themselves, usually grin and give me the "I think I'm going to throw up" look.

Although I believe God enjoys a good romance, I chose this story to paint a different picture. It illustrates God's extravagant love for an individual. I propose God blessed Mandy the way he did to prove to her his ability to minister to *all* her love needs. He gave her a tangible experience demonstrating his love in ways meaningful to her. He confirmed that when she would ask him to minister to the need, the seemingly impossible was indeed possible.

The best methods of meeting a man's or woman's love deficit may look different. However, God can minister to male or female in the best possible ways to fill the love need of the moment with no damage. We just need to look to him to do so.

In reality, God consistently ministers to our love needs in a myriad of ways without our realizing it. We have no idea how many times he has inspired people to bless us in one way or another without our knowing he did so. It would astound us how many "things" we enjoy because God orchestrated circumstances to bless us. He often meets our love needs through other people or things. Unfortunately, because of our lack of knowledge, we often begin to focus on the people or things to meet our needs instead of looking to God and being thankful to him for his gifts.

God loves us. His greatest demonstration of his love for mankind was the birth, life, death, and resurrection of Jesus. However, normally our greatest experiential realizations of God loving us come when our primary focus is loving him with thankful hearts of worship for who he is and what he's done.[3]

Remember my "bad day" story from chapter five? I had no idea going to the refrigerator indicated a love need. But God spoke to me out of the blue and asked, "What are you doing, Deonn?" He got my attention, I got a revelation of my love hunger, and I made a choice to seek him and his help instead of pigging out on food. Then, when I put my focus on him in thankful worship, the love hunger disappeared because I felt his love.

A friend told me recently of a time when God spoke to her unexpectedly during a worship service. "He told me he'd never leave me or abandon me," she said. "I didn't know how much I needed to hear those words until he said them."

Isn't it interesting she heard God speak words of loving comfort she didn't even know she needed *as she worshipped him?* She purposed to love and honor him, yet she walked away tangibly feeling his love.[4]

When we make Jesus the center of our love focus and look to him first and foremost to minister to our needs, we operate according to our created design. In doing so we position ourselves to enjoy all the blessings of love he longs to pour out. Then we know by experience (ginosko) the complete ability of our Creator to minister to our love needs.

## To The Glory Of God

Throughout this book I've built a case for why looking to God to minister to our love needs is the absolute best way to get them met without damaging anyone or anything. I believe everything I've presented is true to the best of my understanding of what Scripture presents and based on my own and others' experiences with God.

Having said that, I believe it's important to clearly communicate another vital truth so you walk away from reading this with the proper perspective. Are you ready? Here it is:

### *This thing called life is not all about us!*

The humanistic philosophy[5] of our world systems permeates the mindsets of many in Christ's church. We've somehow become convinced we deserve to be happy and it's God's job to make us so. We use God and his principles to get what we want or even what we've been told he wants for us. Our motivation? Our happiness. In case you didn't know, God doesn't exist to make us happy, and humanism is not biblical Christianity.[6]

Does God want mankind to be happy? Jesus said he came to give us abundant life.[7] However, in his sermon "Ten Shekels and a Shirt," Paris Reidhead states, "Man's happiness is a by-product of living truth—not the primary product."[8]

When operating according to its created design, everything God made reflects his great glory. When we walk in a love relationship with him, obey his loving guidelines and direction, and choose to respond in love toward our neighbors, we reflect God's glorious goodness on the earth in the greatest possible way. Then, as the Scriptures say, we become lights on a hill who inspire others through our good deeds to glorify the Father.[9]

On the other hand, when we violate our created design, we don't just grieve God's heart and damage ourselves, others, and the earth around us. We also damage the glory of God reflected in his creation. In essence, the darkness of our sin covers the brightness of God's glory which should be reflected through lives lived as God designed. We, therefore, rob God of the greatest glory due him when we choose not to walk in love.[10]

The Father so loved the world he gave his son so whoever believes in him will not perish but have eternal life. Jesus willingly became a man, operated according to his created design as human, humbled himself, and obeyed the Father in all things. Everything Jesus said and did brought glory to God.[11]

Christ is our example. His sacrifice and our acceptance of him as savior and king give us power over sin. Through him we have the ability to choose to walk according to our created design and bring God the glory he deserves through our lives.[12]

When we love God and look to him first and foremost to get our love needs met, he can and will minister to us. He loves us and longs to fulfill every love need he created within us. But something greater than our fulfillment happens when we love him and look to him to meet these needs. The display of God's glory shines brightly through us in ways we won't even recognize most of the time.

Walk in accordance with how God designed us to function best. But don't do it primarily to reap benefits for yourself or even other humans. Again, humanism is not biblical Christianity. To quote Paul, "...whatever you do, do all to the glory of God."[13]

# Final Thoughts

I began this book by sharing one little "ah ha" moment which changed my perspective. Do I always look to God to get my love needs met now? Not perfectly. However, it's a whole lot easier to recognize the "empty places" as love needs than before my "ah ha." Revelation from God is a beautiful thing.

I hope after reading this book you've had your own "ah ha" moments which have changed *your* perspective.

I pray you'll now be able to recognize the cravings in your life for what they are—a desire to have a love need met.

I challenge you to look to God to meet your love needs. From my experience and the experience of others I know, it is the best possible way to get them met without any damage to you or others. And in loving him and looking to him as Lord of all, you'll lessen the grief on his heart, and he will receive the glory he deserves through your life.

Finally, I leave you with an exhortation. I wouldn't apply the following motto to all areas of life because it would be dangerous. But regarding giving God a chance to prove to you his ability to meet you and minister to your love needs without damage, I have one thing to say: "Try it! You'll like it!"[14]

## Questions for Reflection or Discussion

1) In the book summary at the beginning of the chapter, which principle presented has most changed your perspective regarding the topic of love needs? Why?
2) What stood out the most to you from Mandy's story? Why?
3) Under the section entitled "To The Glory Of God," what phrase or concept stood out the most? Why?
4) "Change never occurs through intellectual assent alone. Truth isn't truth learned until it's been applied to our lives." What do these statements mean to you? Ask the

Lord right now to show you what he wants you to do in the coming days to see the truth you've read in this book become the truth you've learned. Write down or share your impressions.

*Father, Son, and Holy Spirit, thank you so much for who you are and how much you love me. I acknowledge you are good, perfect, excellent, complete, and flawless. You are everything I need you to be to fulfill me. I acknowledge this is the truth even if there are places in my thinking or emotions that struggle to believe. Please help me fully believe as I choose to submit myself to you, resist the devil, draw near to you, repent of sin, and purify my heart from being double-minded.*[15]

*I acknowledge my desperate need for you to help me change wrong thinking and bad habit patterns from the past. I want the truth I've read to be the truth I've learned. I ask you now to renew my mind and to help me set my focus "on the things above, not on things that are on the earth."*[16] *Help me get my love needs met in the best possible way—by looking to you to meet them—for your glory. I proclaim in faith, "You can, and you will!" I love you. Amen.*

# Endnotes/Discussion/Appendices

# Endnotes

## Chapter One

[1] *The Amplified Bible, Expanded Edition* (Zondervan Corporation and Lockman Foundation; 1987).

[2] Barbara heard this exercise in 1992 at a seminar conducted by psychologist, speaker, and author, J. Keith Miller.

## Chapter Two

[1] William P. Young, *The Shack,* (Newberry Park, California: Windblown Media, 2007), 124.

[2] Please don't misunderstand. All these things are good, and many are commands of Scripture. However, when done out of a sense of obligation, a desire to perform a duty because we think this is why God created us, we miss the point. On the other hand, when in a healthy, dynamic relationship with our Creator we do these things out of love for him and our fellow man, these commandments aren't a burden (1 John 5:3).

Our purpose for being here is a love relationship with God. When we love God and know by experience how much he loves us, our acts of service come out of love and not just a sense of duty. There's a whole lot more joy in loving and being loved than in serving out of obligation.

[3] Genesis 1:26-27 tells us God created mankind, both male and female, in his image and after his likeness. How are we like God? He can reason and so can we (Isaiah 1:18). He has the ability to choose his actions and so do we (John 15:16; Deuteronomy 30:15-20). He has emotions, and so do we (Genesis 6:6, Jeremiah 31:3).

[4] We all intrinsically know we need love and long to give it. Anyone who says or thinks otherwise has most likely been severely hurt or wounded emotionally. So the real question is did God create us with love needs? If we believe the Bible is true, then we believe God formed our inward parts and wove us together in our mother's womb (Psalm 139:13). If God made us and we have an intrinsic need to love and be loved, then it logically follows God designed us with love needs.

[5] Matthew 22:37-40.

[6] John 3:16.

[7] The Greek word "ginosko" translated "know" in John 17:3 is the same word used in Luke 1:34. Mary asked the angel how she could have a son seeing she did not "ginosko," or know, a man. Mary wasn't speaking of intellectually knowing a man. She meant experientially knowing a man. Really knowing someone means experiencing something with them that goes beyond intellectual understanding alone.

The word intimate means "close familiarity or friendship." [Noah Webster, *American Dictionary of the English Language* (San Francisco, California: Foundation For American Christian Education, 1967)]. An intimate friend is someone with whom we "share our thoughts without reserve. We are real with them." [Ibid.] Eternal life begins and continues within an intimate relationship with God experienced intellectually, emotionally, and even physically at times. It can encompass all of who we are. That's intense, but it's also really, really cool.

[8] James 2:23.

[9] John 15:14.

[10] Proverbs 17:17, Jeremiah 31:3.

[11] Matthew 6:9, 2 Corinthians 6:18, John 1:12, 1 John 3:1-2.

[12] John 14:16, 26; John 16:13.

[13] Ephesians 5:25.

[14] Noah Webster, *American Dictionary of the English Language* (San Francisco, California: Foundation For American Christian Education, 1967).

[15] Betty Swinford, "Show Me Thy Glory," *He's Taking Me To Glory*. Memorial reprinting of Swinford's book copyrighted in 1977. *www.abbalovesus.com/TakingMe2Glory.html* (October 28, 2009).

[16] If we had parents who didn't fulfill their role as God intended, we need to remember God isn't like our earthly parents. Our earthly parents are supposed to attempt to love and care for us, as much as humanly possible, the way God does. All parents will fail sometimes, but God can bring healing and help to every place where those failures wounded us. If our earthly parents failed miserably, we have a heavenly parent who loves us with a never failing love.

[17] God wants to be involved in every part of our lives, including how we utilize finances. He is wiser than we are and knows everything. I learned long ago to give God an opportunity to speak to me regarding what to do with the funds I receive. See the appendix on Hearing God's Voice for more insights on how God speaks.

[18] For the inquiring minds that want to know, my outreach finances all came in, and over time my tuition was completely paid off, as well. God does all things well!

[19] Colossians 1:13-23.

[20] I drafted this paragraph from notes I took during a teaching on relationships by Fran Paris. I give her credit for the concepts expressed.

## Chapter Three

[1] Eugene H. Peterson, *The Message: New Testament, Psalms and Proverbs* (Colorado Springs, Colorado: NavPress in association with Alive Communications, 1995).

[2] Matthew 7:9-11.

[3] Genesis 2:7, Genesis 1:26, Genesis 2.

[4] Genesis 2:19.

[5] Genesis 2:20.

[6] Genesis 2:18.

[7] This statement brings up the question: If God always planned to create male and female, why didn't He create Adam and Eve at the same time? I have a theory. I can't prove it, but since my theory relates to the theme of this book, I want to share it anyway.

I suggest the Trinity created the man first so he would understand experientially their ability to lovingly meet every need of mankind before they introduced another human into the mix. Why? So Adam would protect the human family from looking to other sources outside of God to get their needs met. He knew God could and would meet every need, because God did it for him. Giving him Eve as a helpmeet further proved the point. Adam's role was to then pass on this understanding to future generations as he himself continued to look to God for every provision.

In Eden, one commandment existed: "From any tree of the garden you may eat freely; but from the tree of the knowledge of good and evil you shall not eat, for in the day that you eat from it you shall surely die" (Genesis 2:16-17). The serpent crept into the garden to beguile humanity to look to something other than God to meet their emotional needs. Be assured, the need Adam and Eve sought to meet through their disobedience wasn't physical. They could eat from any tree they wanted to except the one they chose (Genesis 2:16).

I surmise Adam and Eve attempted to meet a legitimate love need through their disobedience. Perhaps they wanted a sense of importance or value. "For God knows that in the day you eat from it your eyes will be opened, and you will be like God..." (Genesis 3:5). Perhaps for Adam his need for acceptance from the woman motivated him to stand there, listen to the serpent's lies without speaking a word, and then eat the forbidden fruit handed him by his wife (Genesis 3:6). In fact, God later said, "Because you have listened to the voice of your wife...cursed is the ground because of you..." (Genesis 3:17).

Finally, consider this: Eve ate the forbidden fruit first. However, Scripture never teaches sin entered the world through Eve. It states plainly sin entered the world through Adam (Romans 5:12). The serpent deceived Eve, but not Adam. He didn't protect, he didn't say a word of what he'd experienced of God's ability to meet every need, and he ate the fruit knowing full well doing so meant he disobeyed the one who'd provided for *all* his needs. Adam experientially knew better but, I contend, tried to fill a legitimate love need in the wrong way anyway. The rest is history.

## Chapter Four

[1] Gary D. Chapman, *The Five Love Languages* (Chicago, Illinois: Northfield Publishing, 1995), 21.

[2] Though I searched via the Internet to find him/her, I do not know the author of this drama. I've met others from around the country who've performed it with several different variations, and no one knew where it originated. I apologize for not being able to credit the author by name. May he or she receive rewards in heaven for the impact the drama's message has had on hundreds of lives. Amen!

[3] He acts as if shoveling and throwing dirt over his shoulder and then salutes.

[4] Colossians 3:23-24.

[5] The motions for this one are classic. While delivering the "see me," the actor put his right hand under his left armpit and moved his arm as if trying to make the "passing gas" noise. During the "notice me," he acted like he picked his nose. When he delivered the "don't you want to know me?" he stood on one foot, kicking the other foot in the air and moving his hands, palms up, back and forth. His facial expression screamed, "I'm cool, don't you think?"

[6] The player pretends to drink something, acts as if smoking something, then put hands around his/her neck as if choking.

[7] The actor starts with a strongman stance, rubs right hand over left arm on the part about being tan, and then points to himself on "be" and points to the audience with a wink during "your macho man."

[8] She starts by making a halo over her head with her hands, then points to her "dimples" on both cheeks, and lastly lifts her right foot and points to it repeatedly with both index fingers in time with the rhythm of the phrase.

[9] See Chapter 7 for more information on emotional dependency.

[10] Ephesians 4:32.

[11] 2 Timothy 1:7.

[12] 1 John 4:18.

[13] The player hugs herself, blows a kiss, and then turns her back to the audience and rubs her hands up and down her arms to appear as though someone else is caressing her.

[14] In Gary Chapman's book, *The Five Love Languages,* he wrote a whole chapter devoted to a discussion regarding individuals whose primary way of communicating love is physical touch. (Chapman, 103-116.) I have friends who like touching me because they are communicating love, not because they are looking to me to meet their love needs. Their touches are healthy and appropriate. I'm not talking about these people. The text refers to people who are so emotionally needy, they pursue physical relationships because it's the only place they feel secure, valued, comforted, and/or accepted.

[15] If using this material in a discussion group, a general prayer for all those mentioned by the participants may be appropriate. Or, if time allows, have those assembled get in groups of two or three to share the names of those who came to mind. Then have them pray together for those mentioned.

## Chapter Five

[1] *The Amplified Bible, Expanded Edition* (Zondervan Corporation and Lockman Foundation; 1987).

[2] I credit Larry Allen with the creation of this analogy. I heard him use it back in the early 1990s. I've simply created a few more details to make the illustration a little more real and personal for the reader. Thanks, Larry, for giving me permission to use it here.

[3] Romans 3:23.

[4] Samson's story is recounted in Judges chapters 13 – 16. Any place in this section on Samson where any of his story is told, you may refer to these chapters to corroborate the accuracy of my statements.

[5] Some may ask, "How do you know this is a true statement? There is no place in Judges where it tells us God grieved over Samson's bad choices."

The question is a good one. I freely admit I am making an assumption when I conclude God cried with grief over his damaged creation. However, when I consider God's deep love for mankind communicated throughout the Scripture and the many times it says He grieved over sin's resulting effects, I believe my assumption is at least plausible. When I think about Jesus' weeping over Jerusalem, his agonizing death on a cross to redeem mankind from the power of sin, and what I felt as I cried with grief over a foolish generation in a Minneapolis nightclub, I believe my assumption is probable. Feel free to disagree.

[6] The story of Saul is primarily told from 1 Samuel 9 – 31. Because Saul's life is woven throughout these chapters, at the end of each paragraph where I talk about specifics of his life, the paragraph will have an endnote. In each endnote, I will note the references used.

[7] 1 Samuel 9:15, 10:1-13.

[8] 1 Samuel 13:8-14.

[9] 1 Samuel 15 – specific references to verses 24 and 26.

[10] 1 Samuel 18:10-16.

[11] The story of David and Bathsheba can be found in 2 Samuel 11. Since the majority of this section on David revolves around this story, you may read this chapter to verify my statements.

[12] 2 Samuel 11:27.

[13] Max Lucado, *Facing Your Giants* (Nashville, Tennessee: W. Publishing Group, a division of Thomas Nelson, 2006), 145.

## Chapter Six

[1] *The Holy Bible: New Living Translation; Second Edition* (Wheaton, Illinois: Tyndale House Publishers and Tyndale Charitable Trust, 2004).

[2] Craig Musseau, *Arms of Love*, Mercy/Vineyard Publishing, 1991. (This song originally debuted on the CD *Touching The Father's Heart 11* entitled *I Bow Down*. The CD I listened to is entitled *Psalms – Volume 4* released by Vineyard Music in 1994.)

[3] I acknowledge many other serious food addictions exist, but I focus on compulsive overeating in this chapter because I've seen its destructive results up close. I chose to highlight the problem I've observed the most.

[4] Dr. Frank Minirth, Dr. Paul Meier, Dr. Robert Hemfelt, Dr. Sharon Sneed, and Don Hawkins; *Love Hunger–Recovery from Food Addiction* (United States of America: The Ballantine Publishing Group, 1991) 13.

[5] Ibid.

[6] Author Unknown, "Are You A Compulsive Overeater?" *Is OA For You? Overeaters Anonymous: www.oa.org/new-to-oa/is-oa-for-you.php* (October 27, 2009).

[7] Author Unknown, "Eating Disorders are Widespread and Destructive" *More Information on Eating Disorders. A Place of Hope: www.aplaceofhope.com/more_eating.html* (December 1, 2008).

[8] Author Unknown, "Compulsive Overeating Treatment" *Articles. ChristiaNet – The Worldwide Christian Marketplace: www.christianet.com/anorexia/compulsiveovereatingtreatment.ht m* (December 1, 2008).

[9] *The Holy Bible: New Living Translation.*

[10] Since the theme of this book is love needs, I've only skimmed the topic of eating disorders to show the connection between the two. However, I believe many who read this book really struggle in this area. So, "Felicia" and her Christian counselor recommend the following books for those who want more information on compulsive overeating: *Love Hunger* by Minirth & Meier, *Fat is a Family Affair* by Genene Roth, and *Why Weight?* by Genene Roth. The websites referenced in this chapter also have much more information regarding various eating disorders and recommendations of places to receive help getting healing from them.

If you struggle with an eating disorder of any kind, please cry out to God for deliverance, but also tell a mature, trusted person in your life about your struggles. It's important you don't try to do this on your own. You need someone, or many others, to assist you in finding help and to pray for you through the process. And consider this, the devil wants you to believe it's hopeless and you can't be helped, but he's a liar (John 8:44). Nothing is impossible with God (Luke 1:37). He truly can minister to every need of your life when you ask him for help and obey his direction.

## Chapter Seven

[1] Young, *The Shack,* 95.

[2] Lori Thorkelson, "Emotional Dependency – A Threat To Close Friendships – Part 1", PDF/Adobe Acrobat, *Google: www.google.com/#hl=en&source=hp&q=emotional+dependency+l ori+thorkelson&aq=8m&aqi+g8g-m1&oq=Lori&Thor&fp=38boec042cf1835a* (October 28, 2009).

[3] Ibid.

[4] Steve Prokopchak, "Defining Emotional Dependency", *Emotional Dependency in Cells – How To Identify and Break the Bondage of Dependent Relationships.* Microsoft Word Document. *Tri-Lakes Chapel: www.trilakeschapel.org/library/Emotional.doc* (October 28, 2009).

[5] Ibid.

[6] Thorkelson, *Emotional Dependency.*

[7] As I mentioned in endnote number nine in chapter four, not all physical touch is unhealthy. However, what I'm talking about here are caresses while gazing into the other person's eyes, long drawn out hugs, wanting to hold hands to feel connected all the time, laying down while holding each other, playing with the other person's hair, etc. These physical connections are often unhealthy. In same sex friendships or parent/child relationships, these kinds of physical touches can at times be motivated by trying to get love needs met in a wrong way. Caution is advised.

Even in guy/girl dating relationships, if we always think about being with the other person in these physical ways predominantly, then perhaps the relationship is headed down an unhealthy path. Do we care about the person or just the way they bring comfort, security, acceptance, and value to us through physical contact?

Even if the physical contact isn't unhealthy for us and we have no "love need" we are trying to meet through the contact, is it healthy for the other person? Only God and the other person truly know. However, sometimes the other person won't feel comfortable sharing what they feel because of embarrassment or shame. It's important to stay sensitive to the Holy Spirit in our relationships.

A friend of mine told me a story to illustrate this point. During her engagement, she and her fiancé were traveling some place by car. As they chatted, she had her arm laid across the back of the seat. Without really thinking about it, she reached up and started running her hand through his hair and began rubbing his head as she continued talking and telling him a story. The Holy Spirit spoke to her and said, "Stop it!" She gently removed her hand knowing God wouldn't have spoken so insistently if it weren't important. Later she asked the Lord what that was all about. He said, "Your physical touches were stirring things in him that were not appropriate outside the context of marriage. You needed to stop to make it easier for him to rein in his thoughts and emotions which your touch triggered."

Loving, appropriate touch is important for humans. We need it. I'm told scientists have observed giving and receiving hugs help people stay healthier. However, we need to be careful to check our own motivations and be sensitive to the Holy Spirit regarding displays of physical affection to those we love. Please don't be afraid to touch someone with brief hugs, encouraging touches, etc. My point is when we look to a person to receive those touches for comfort instead of looking to God for comfort, damage may eventually occur.

[8] Thorkelson, *Emotional Dependency;* and Prokopchak, *Defining Emotional Dependency.*

[9] God never intended us to meet every emotional need of the people we love. That's his job. He might allow us to help, but it's not our job. We can't fix everything for people, only he can. If we try, we will become entangled in a snare of pressure, stress, and fear. The best we can do is continually point the person we love to Jesus and allow God to show the other person his ability to take care of them. Sometimes we need to get out of the way, even if it hurts, so the person has the opportunity to turn to the Lord.

However, if dependency is happening in a marriage relationship, don't back away from the marriage. Caution and counsel is necessary to help the dependent person receive healing. The non-dependent spouse should seek help for them as a couple from professional Christian counselors and maintain clear, honest, loving communication throughout the process.

[10] I did a word study on James 1. Verse 15 says, "Then when lust has conceived, it gives birth to sin; and when sin is accomplished, it brings forth death."

My amplified rendition of the verse based on my word study reads like this: "Then when his own desire for what is forbidden is indulged in, it births a violation of the Divine Law (the law of love) in thought or act, and when the violation of the Divine Law (of love) in thought or act is accomplished, **it births a misery of the soul**."

I cried for an hour. My sin, looking to a person to meet my love needs instead of God, birthed a misery of the soul. Violating our created design will *always* eventually lead to a misery of the soul.

[11] *The Amplified Bible, Expanded Edition.*

[12] Most people consider love to be a feeling, but emotions don't exist because someone commanded them to exist. BE SAD! Go ahead, BE SAD right now. I command it! In a few moments you

might be able to think a sad thought and work up an emotion, but God's commands aren't about working up an emotion.

The greatest commandments are to love God with everything in us and love our neighbor as ourselves (Matthew 22:37-39). Jesus is not commanding an emotion but a choice to honor him and others by walking in the principles of love laid out by his example and the Scriptures that describe love. When we apply the principles, warm feelings may follow, but it's not the feelings Jesus commanded. And when we choose the most loving thing for God, others, and ourselves, Scripture says we obey all commanded by the law and the prophets (Matthew 22:40). Love is the Divine Law.

[13] Matthew 5:44, Luke 6:35.

## Chapter Eight

[1] John 16:8.

[2] 1 Timothy 4:1-2, Ephesians 4:17-21.

[3] 1 John 1:9, 1 John 2:1-2.

[4] My experience of deliverance from a lustful stronghold of masturbation may be confusing to some. Many teach that Christians can't be possessed by the devil therefore Christians don't need deliverance. I agree and disagree with this teaching. Let me explain.

I agree Christians can't be possessed because possession indicates ownership. When we truly give our lives to Jesus, we've given him the right of ownership. We are his (1 Corinthians 6:19-20). The devil cannot possess us because, as an act of our will, we already belong to Jesus.

However, I disagree this means Christians don't need deliverance. Demonic strongholds can exist based on continuous involvement in sinful activities before or after conversion. Because of my habitual participation in the lustful sin of masturbation over a number of years, the enemy held me captive. When in captivity, it's a lot harder to say no when the temptation to sin arises. Let me be clear, though. I was responsible for my wrong choices to sin—the devil didn't MAKE me do it—but being in bondage to sin made it more difficult not to sin. I needed freedom in this area. Once the enemy, the python in the picture, was vanquished, kicked out, removed, I had greater ease to say no to temptations in this realm.

I believe Christians often struggle with past sins because they still have strongholds of sin in certain areas. They've been forgiven, they belong to God, but the demonic strongholds from the past haven't been dealt with yet. They need deliverance so it's easier to say no when temptation comes their way.

Do we need to cast out demons every time someone struggles with sinful behavior? Not necessarily. We can't assume every struggle with sin results because of demonic strongholds. Scripture teaches destructive results also happen because of lack of knowledge (Hosea 4:6). Many of our choices to sin are rooted in lies we believe about God, ourselves, and others. All of us need our minds renewed and our "stinking thinking" exposed by the truth of God's Word. Experientially knowing truth sets us free. Counseling, teaching, and prayer from mature believers can often help us see our wrong thinking, help us believe the truth, and more easily resist temptation. But, as in my case, if we have heard and believed truth, prayed our guts out, sincerely hated the sin, and still keep on screwing up anyway, then perhaps a demonic stronghold needs to be dealt with.

For more understanding concerning spiritual warfare, I highly recommend two books:

- "Spiritual Warfare For Every Christian" by Dean Sherman, and published by YWAM Publishing, presents wonderful, practical truths regarding spiritual warfare. I suggest reading this one first to get a good, scriptural foundation on the topic.
- "Christian Set Yourself Free" by Graham and Shirley Powell, published by Sovereign World Publishers and distributed by Renew Books, provides a scriptural and, in my opinion, balanced approach to the topic of deliverance.

A last thought here. Don't worry about whether you have demonic strongholds or need deliverance. You don't need to walk in fear. God's perfect love drives fear away. Rest in God's love for you. He'll show you where you need your thinking renewed or deliverance from strongholds. You focus on loving him with all your heart, mind, soul, and strength, and he'll work in you everything you need—one step at a time.

[5] Obviously, this chapter sub-topic has a double meaning. It refers to our literal bodies but also the body of Christ at large.

[6] Genesis 1:31.

[7] Hebrews 13:4.

[8] Grantly Morris, "Masturbation: Moral Quicksand or God's Provision for Those Without Adequate Partners?" *Masturbation and the Bible: Towards a Christian View of Sexual Self-Stimulation: Internet Evangelism and Teaching: www.net-burst.net/sexuality/masturbate.htm* (December 3, 2008).

Morris bases the quoted statements in the first paragraph on Genesis 1:28 where God commanded the male and female to "be fruitful and multiply." Sexual intercourse between the husband and wife produces offspring within the boundaries of a marriage relationship as God created marriage to be from the beginning—one man and one woman for a lifetime.

The superglue analogy comes from Genesis 2:24 where Adam states, "For this cause a man shall leave his father and his mother, and shall cleave to his wife; and they shall become one flesh." The word translated *cleave* is the Hebrew word *dabaq* (pronounced daw-bak'). It means "to stick close to, to cling, to stay, to be joined together." (From the free online software *Online Bible Version 1.0.4* by Ken Hamel, [Woodside Bible Fellowship, 1992]).

It's logical to assume God created this joining (sexual intercourse) to be pleasurable to assist in the desire to stay with the person joined to and to continue coming back for more joining so as to bring forth more fruit. But to engage in this act of cleaving and to separate or cut off from the one to whom you've joined is damaging. It's like trying to take apart something that's been superglued—the two parts are never the same again. That's why Jesus admonished against the idea of divorce, with only few exceptions, by saying, "...What God has joined together, let no man separate" (Matthew 19:6).

In the second paragraph Morris assumes sex was also created by God as a way to express marital love that focuses on giving to the other person. This concept of giving is central to the idea of love. "For God so loved the world that he gave..." (John 3:16). As I emphasized in Chapter 3, love longs to give. So, ultimately if true love is involved in sexual activities, both parties should be focused on giving to the one they love, not on what they are getting out of it. And, as has already been stated, this giving is to be done only in the context of a marriage relationship because it is the only relationship in which God designed for sex to take place.

God doesn't want those he created violating their design. Engaging in sexual activities outside of God's created guidelines is sin and will eventually lead to someone being hurt—emotionally, physically, spiritually, and mentally. And the one who grieves the most when that happens is God.

[9] Rob Bell, *Sex God* (Grand Rapids, Michigan: Zondervan, 2007) 164.

[10] *New International Version of the Holy Bible,* 7th Printing (Grand Rapids, Michigan: Zondervan, 1986).

[11] Mike Genung, "Statistics and Information on Pornography in the USA", *Safe Families – Keeping Children Safe Online.* Copyright 2005. *Blazing Grace: www.blazinggrace.org/cms/bg/pornstats* (December 3, 2008).

[12] When I first experienced deliverance from the stronghold of masturbation, my pastoral care leader told me freedom didn't mean an end to temptation. Because of the physical sensations I'd experienced over many years, she warned there would be times I'd be tempted to engage in this sexual act again. She encouraged me to remember the bondage I'd been in before and to CHOOSE to say yes to God and no to the enemy and my fleshly desires. She said it would be easier to say no now that the stronghold was gone.

In the last two decades I've been tempted to masturbate many times. But I remember the misery of soul which bound me for years, and I've chosen to "take my thoughts captive to the obedience of Christ" (2 Corinthians 10:5). I'm still free from the stronghold and grateful to the Lord for his deliverance.

As wonderful as it is to give this report, I must say something here about dreams.

I cannot say I haven't ever again experienced an orgasm. Though it doesn't happen often, I've had dreams that stimulated me and produced physical responses in my body. (When males experience something like this, it's often called a "wet" dream because they ejaculate.)

Because of our limited control over our dreams, I don't believe having a dream that produces orgasm or ejaculation necessarily constitutes sin on our part. Sin is a choice to violate the law of love. I don't know about you, but I don't choose my dreams; they just happen.

However, the things we look at and think about can influence what we dream. If we've recently viewed sexual material, engaged in sexual conversations, or listened to suggestive music and then have a sexual dream, perhaps repentance is in order. If, on the other hand, we've not involved ourselves in these activities and we have a sexual dream, I don't believe sin has occurred. God looks at the heart, not the outward appearance (1 Samuel 16:7).

If you ever have a sexual dream and God doesn't show you a choice you made that influenced having the dream, I suggest you do the following. When you are fully awake, resist the enemy's accusations and submit yourself to the Holy Spirit. Ask him to wash your mind and spirit from any residual feelings of guilt, shame, or lust deposited through the dream. He will meet you and encourage your heart for the day ahead. How do I know? Because he does it for me, and he is no respecter of persons (Acts 10:34).

[13] Francis Frangipane, *Holiness, Truth, and the Presence of God*, Fourteenth Printing (Cedar Rapids, Iowa: Arrow Publications, 1996) 26.

[14] If the chapter is to be discussed in a group setting and it's a mixed group, it may be wise to have the men and women meet

separately for the discussion. Ask the Lord what is best for your group dynamic.

There may be varied opinions within the group regarding this topic, but it is essential Scripture be the standard. If someone becomes argumentative, suggest meeting with them at another time. Also, I suggest the leaders be prepared for personal ministry to the group. Most likely several in the group struggle with sexual sins.

In this book I've tried to correlate a connection between sexual sins and trying to get love needs met in a wrong way. Many other books or websites will be more helpful to further delve into the specific topic of sexual sins. I'd suggest some of the sites referenced in this chapter as a place to start.

[15] HealingForTheSoul, "Struggling With Pornography? There's Hope...", *Exodus Youth: Finding True Freedom*. October 16, 2008. *Exodus Youth: www.exodusyouth.net/2008/10/16/struggling-with-pornography-theres-hope/* (November 19, 2008).

## Chapter Nine

[1] Craig S. Hill and Earl Pitts, *Wealth, Riches and Money*, (Littleton, Colorado: Family Foundations Publishing, 2001) 3.

[2] 1 Timothy 6:10.

[3] Hill and Pitts, *Wealth, Riches and Money*, 3.

[4] I'd been saving for a new car for a few years. I desired no debt, so I'd committed myself to not purchase until I could pay for it up front. Most godly financial advisors recommend this course of action. I considered this a reasonable, logical, intelligent plan.

While driving one day, an impression came to my mind out of nowhere to purchase a car NOW. I reasoned the thought away saying, "I won't go into debt. I only have half the money needed to buy what I want. This can't be God." However, the thought wouldn't go away, so I began praying about it. I felt like God spoke to me to purchase the car now and he would pay it off in a year.

So, I bought the exact car I wanted, still owing $10,000 on it after paying the down payment. Two days before the one-year anniversary of picking up my car, I made the last payment. God fulfilled his promise with two days to spare.

In that year I had to travel extensively because of ministry obligations. My other car would not have made those trips without problems. I was able to give my other car to my niece who merely drove the car locally to work and back.

Obeying God's direction made no sense at the time, but looking back, it makes complete sense. I made sure I had confirmations from the Lord before I went forward with the purchase, but when I obeyed, blessings followed for me and others. Obedience to God is intelligent.

[5] James Strong, LL.D., D.T.D., *The Strongest Strong's Exhaustive Concordance of the Bible,* Fully Revised and Corrected by John R. Kohlenberger III and James A. Swanson (Grand Rapids, Michigan: Zondervan, 2001) Greek Dictionary Index #1343.

In Matthew 23 Jesus made it clear to the Pharisees that God considers our actions in agreement with his standards and relationship with him proper based on heart motive, not just external action. In verses 25-28 he told them they cleaned themselves up on the outside so they looked good to men, but on the inside they were filthy and dead. Their "noble" actions may have fooled men, but they didn't fool God. Jesus exhorted them to clean the inside so the outside would really be clean and not hypocritical.

Righteousness and seeking God's righteousness should work from the internal heart motivations of love for God and others and manifest in external actions. Does that mean we should stop doing good things if our motives are wrong? Absolutely not! Choose to do good things even if your motivations aren't yet pure, but also choose to allow God to help you change your motives. We can't do it without him, but with him all things are possible (John 15:5, Matthew 19:26).

[6] Luke 1:37.

## Chapter Ten

[1] The "guild" is the other people with whom individual gamers play the role-playing games.

[2] Dancing - Exodus 15:20; Drama - Ezekiel 4; Story telling - Luke 14:7; Fishing - John 21; 1 Racing - Corinthians 9:24-27.

[3] Sexual sin – 1 Corinthians 6:18, 2 Timothy 2:22; Fear – 1 John 4:18; Unwholesome, silly talk – Ephesians 5:4.

[4] Blind spots are called blind spots because the one who has them can't see them. If anyone voices a concern about an aspect of our lives, the smart thing to do is to thank them for their insights and let them know we'll ask God about it. Then, we should ask God about it. If God shows us there is any truth in the concern, we should respond to God as he directs. If there isn't, we ought to pray a prayer of blessing over the person and thank God for people who care about us—even when they are wrong.

When I've responded to people's concerns in the way just described, it's always been beneficial. Sometimes what they shared held truth, and I grew from the experience as I responded to the Lord. Sometimes I felt no conviction from the Lord regarding what they told me, but the exercise in humility helped me grow.

On the other hand, when concerns were voiced and I puffed up with pride, rationalizing my actions and ignoring what they shared, I always lost. God resists the proud but gives grace to the humble (1 Peter 5:5).

## Chapter Eleven

[1] The Pharisees in Scripture are prime examples of this truth. They kept all the required laws of the Jewish religion and added some traditions of their own, as well. Yet Jesus told them they were of their father, the devil (John 8:42-47). They didn't know God or really love him. They simply did their duty to look good in the eyes of the world (Matthew 23:5). Fulfilling external religious duties, even good ones, is not the same as having a relationship with the creator of the universe. However, as I've already stated in an earlier chapter, the answer is not to stop doing good things. The answer is to open your heart to the loving creator of all things and let him be father and friend.

[2] *Holy Bible – New King James Version* (Nashville, Tennessee: Thomas Nelson, 1982).

The Greek word translated "willing" in the New King James is the word "boulomai." Strong's Concordance (Greek index reference # 1014) says it means "to wish, will, desire; to choose, determine, plan." God did not wish, will, desire, choose, determine, or plan for anyone to perish. According to this verse, his wish, will, desire, choice, determination, and plan is for everyone to repent of their sin.

[3] 1 Timothy 2:1-2, 1 Thessalonians 5:17, Matthew 5:44.

[4] Ezekiel 22:30 indicates God desired to show mercy to Israel when their actions clearly deserved judgment. However, he could not find a man among them to "stand in the gap" (pray or intercede) on behalf of the Israelites.

The question then becomes, if God wanted to extend mercy, why did he need a man to pray for it? I believe Dutch Sheets in chapter two of his book *Intercessory Prayer* (Ventura, California: Regal Books, 1996) presents a compelling, logical answer. In his sovereignty,* the all-powerful God made a decision in the beginning. God gave men dominion (rulership, guardianship) over the earth (Genesis 1:26-28, Psalm 8:6, Psalm 115:16). Mankind became his representatives or stewards here. He decided to limit himself regarding what happens on earth to working through men and women who walked in relationship with him.

Why would he do that? Sheets suggests most good fathers enjoy working with their kids in the family business. Though God assigned responsibility of the earth to mankind, he loves us to look to him to find out how it should best work. (We've already established the creator of something knows best how it should function.) In our relationship with God, when we find God's will for any given situation on earth and ask him to bring it about, we open the door for him to move to accomplish it. Prayer is an amazing part of our relationship with the Lord. It's our privilege and responsibility in seeing "the family business" flourish.

Note: *Intercessory Prayer* has a lot of word studies on the original meanings of scriptures. Though an excellent book, I'd recommend another of his books for those not wanting that kind of in depth analysis. *The Beginner's Guide To Intercession* (Ann Arbor, Michigan: Servant Publications, 2001) has similar principles presented but is much more practical for those wanting to learn the basic purposes and power of intercessory prayer. Good stuff!

*Sovereign = supreme ruler or authority to whom all other authorities must answer. (My definition based on concepts presented in Noah Webster's 1828 *American Dictionary of the English Language*.)

[5] Notice I didn't say causes. Some people think God causes all things. Others believe God causes all the good things and the devil causes all the bad. The reality is God and the devil are influences in our individual lives—not causes. God created mankind with an ability to choose (Genesis 2-3). The Lord lovingly attempts to influence us to operate according to our created design because he loves us. The enemy attempts to influence us through lies and deception to violate our created design because he hates God and us. However, we choose our course of action. Therefore we are responsible and accountable for our choices.

Having said that, I'm not saying God doesn't cause some things. There are some rare occasions in Scripture when God overrode a person's will to bring about his purposes and destiny for a nation. For example, in Exodus 7-12 he hardened Pharaoh's heart five out of ten times — Pharaoh hardened his own heart the other five times. Because God is completely just and loving, if he does cause an attitude or action to bring about his destiny for a nation, he will not hold that individual responsible or accountable for that attitude or action. If something is caused, it is not responsible. However, the individual would be accountable and responsible for all the attitudes and actions they chose.

[6] My friend Kip Gaines first mentioned these five influences to me. I have no idea where he got his understanding of these principles, but I give him credit for at the very least teaching me so I could teach you. Thanks, Kip!

No believer would argue against God being an influence in our lives. Unfortunately, a lot of believers think he's the only influence. Scripture doesn't substantiate this notion. Consider the following list of references concerning each of the influences mentioned.

- God - Genesis 12, Exodus 3, Acts 8.
- Angels – Good – Psalm 91:11-12, 2 Kings 6:15-17, Daniel 8:16; Bad – Revelation 12:9, John 10:10, 1 Timothy 4:1.
- Other peoples' choices – Good – Genesis 24, Nehemiah 1-2, Acts 10; Bad - Genesis 34, 2 Samuel 11, Acts 7.
- Our own choices – Good – Exodus 14, Joshua 6, Luke 10; Bad – Judges 16, Genesis 16, 2 Samuel 13.
- Circumstances – (Accidents) – 2 Samuel 4:4, Numbers 35.

[7] James 4:6-9, Ephesians. 1-6.

[8] Matthew 22:37-40, Matthew 5:44, John 13:34-35.

[9] John 3:16, Romans 10:13, 2 Peter 3:9.

[10] See "Hearing God's Voice" in the appendix for more information.

[11] Isaiah 1:18, Matthew 11:28-30, Psalm 27:8.

[12] 2 Chronicles 16:9, 1 Peter 5:7.

[13] Scripture lists dozens of examples to prove the point. I've given you five.

- Moses saw the bush that burned but wasn't consumed, and God spoke to him from the bush (Exodus 3).
- Isaiah saw the Lord and was so moved by the glory of his presence, he recognized his own sinfulness and repented.

He then felt the touch of a coal cleansing his lips and heard the Lord ask him a question (Isaiah 6).

- God spoke to Jeremiah about his destiny and then touched him on the mouth declaring, "Behold, I have put My words in your mouth" (Jeremiah 1).
- John was "in the Spirit on the Lord's day" and he saw Jesus. Jesus spoke to him and touched him (Revelation 1).
- A woman who'd hemorrhaged for twelve years touched Jesus and the hemorrhaging stopped immediately (Luke 8:43-48).

[14] Mark 10:45, Mark 10:43-44, Hebrews 4:14.

[15] See appendix entitled "The Character of God" for more information.

[16] Chapman, *The Five Love Languages,* 38.

[17] Peterson, *The Message,* 2 Corinthians 10:5.

## Chapter Twelve

[1] Joy Dawson, *Intimate Friendship with God,* (Old Tappen, New Jersey: Chosen Books, 1986) 18.

[2] John 8:31-36.

[3] A few times in my life the love demonstrated by others toward me overwhelmed me with a sense of God's love for me. I knew beyond a shadow of a doubt their gifts or actions toward me were God-inspired to express more than just their love for me but God's love, as well. But it's normally when I've had a God-focused time of prayer, worship, and/or thanksgiving when God's demonstrations of love have been most amazing. "In Thy presence is fullness of joy…" (Psalm 16:11)

[4] I could tell numerous stories from my own life of how God ministered to me in incredible ways as I worshipped him. He's given scriptures to encourage, pictures in my mind's eye to give me a sense of his nearness, words of love to comfort, and even a physical sense of his presence and power to remind me he's very real. I worship him because he's worthy, not for what *I* get out of it. However, when I've genuinely expressed my love to him in worship, he almost always makes sure I walk away knowing he loves me back.

[5] Humanism – "A philosophy that asserts the dignity and worth of man and his capacity for self-realization through reason and that often rejects supernaturalism." Noah Webster, *Webster's New Collegiate Dictionary,* Henry Bosley Woolf – Editor in Chief, (Springfield, Massachusetts: G. & C. Merriam Company, 1976), 556.

Humanism as a philosophy most often rejects God's existence or God's interaction with mankind. Man is the measure of all things. God, if he even exists, has nothing to do with us.

[6] According to Austin Cline, [*Humanism in Ancient Greece: History of Humanism With Ancient Greek Philosophers,* About.com: Agnosticism/Atheism, *About.com: www.*atheism.about.com/od/abouthumanism/a/ancientgreece.ht m?p=1 (November 24, 2009)], the term "humanism" was not applied to a philosophy or a belief system until the European Renaissance in the 1800s. However, the ideas and attitudes of humanism can be discovered in many forgotten manuscripts from ancient Greece.

Protagoras, a Greek philosopher and teacher who lived approximately 500 years before Christ, is one of the first who wrote some of the beginnings of "humanist" doctrine from which many others took their views. His philosophy exhibited two important features that remain central to humanism today.

1)  Man is the measure (or center) of all things.  In other words, it is not to the gods that we should look when establishing standards, but instead to ourselves. We should do what is right in our own eyes.
2)  He regarded traditional religious beliefs and traditional "gods" with doubt. He didn't know if any god/gods existed, but even if they did, he didn't see they had much to do with human life. He believed and promoted the concept man is the answer for man's problems if there is an answer at all.

Socrates, Aristotle, Democritus, and Epicurus were other Greek philosophers who also tried to analyze the workings of the world from a naturalistic (man centered, stuff just is and got here by itself) perspective rather than as the actions of "the gods."

In his sermon "Ten Shekels and a Shirt," Paris Reidheid discusses how the philosophy of humanism surged to popularity in the 1800s after the great European revivals with Whitfield and Wesley. [Paris Reidhead, "Ten Shekels and a Shirt," *Paris Reidhead Bible Teaching Ministries: www.parisreidheadbibleteachingministries.org/tenshekels.shtml* (November 24, 2009)].

The humanists in Europe had studied and adhered to these Greek philosophies and began a frontal attack on the Word of God around 1850. The prevailing philosophy in science, art, music, theater, fashion, business, education, etc. was humanistic at its core. It was a commonly held belief among these Renaissance thinkers that the end goal of life was to get all the happiness you can, any way you can, for as long as you can, because this is all there is. Man is the center of all things, and the end of all being is the happiness of man. Find happiness, you've found salvation and are successful.

Surrounded by a culture permeated with humanistic thought, the Christian ranks became divided into two extremes.

1) Liberal Christians – They accepted a humanistic slant regarding religion. They basically said, "We don't know if there is a heaven or a hell, but we can have and do some good stuff here for 70 years. Join our club, and we'll make you feel good about yourself. We'll give you some nice things to help your trip be more enjoyable. We'll share some messages with simple concepts from the Bible, or any other source we decide will help, just to make you feel good. We'll develop programs to get you off drugs and alcohol and help you with food and clothing. God wants all men everywhere to be happy, and we're here to help make that happen."

2) Fundamentalist Christians – They totally rejected the cultural perspective and held to a strict belief in the absolute truth of the Word of God. As wicked sinners, mankind needed a savior and God provided one—Jesus. Give your life to God through Jesus, and leave your life of sin. Jesus will redeem you and you can spend eternity with Him. Then you'll be happy. Don't worry about the here and now—you'll be happy later.

The second-generation fundamentalists taught a slightly different version. They said, "This is how you become a fundamentalist. Believe this and go to heaven. Rules and regulations get you where you want to go. Follow them and be happy for eternity."

The third generation fundamentalists said, "If you simply give intellectual assent to a few statements of doctrine, and say yes in the appropriate places, we'll give you a pat on the back and you'll be saved from hell and on your way to heaven." In other words, say you believe in God and Jesus, say the sinner's prayer, and then you're in.

Boiling down both extremes, we see the liberals were about social change and social programs to make humans happy while they were alive. The fundamentalists, on the other hand, worked hard to help everyone be happy when they died. Both were an appeal to selfishness. Both made mankind's happiness the ultimate goal. Both made God, religion, Jesus, and the Bible a means to the end goal of humanity's happiness. Both were humanistic.

In his sermon on humanism Mr. Reidhead proclaimed, "Humanism is the most destructive philosophy to creep up from the pit of hell. It is in TOTAL contrast to Christianity...True believers live the principle: 'God is the center of all things. The end of all being is the glory of God. I live only and ever in worship and adoration to Him because the Lamb that was slain is worthy to receive the reward of His suffering.'"

I agree with Mr. Reidhead.

[7] John 10:10.

[8] Reidhead, *Ten Shekels and a Shirt*.

[9] Matthew 5:14-16.

[10] Matthew 5:13-16 communicates this concept. Jesus implies through word pictures, "I call you salt. Be salty so men will glorify my Father. I call you light, so don't hide the light. Let it shine so men will glorify my Father. If you violate your design and hide the light or lose your saltiness, my Father will not receive the full glory he deserves."

[11] John 3:16, Philippians 2 5-11, John 17:4-5.

[12] 1 Peter 2:21-25, Romans 8.

[13] 1 Corinthians 10:31.

[14] This slogan became popular through a television advertisement for Alka-Seltzer back in the early 1970s. The ad agency "Wells Rich Greene" created it.

Stuart Elliott, "Try It: You Liked It Once, and Alka-Seltzer Hopes You Do Again," *The New York Times,* Published June 19, 2006, *The New York Times Media and Advertising: www.nytimes.com/2006/19/business/media/19adco.html* (December 2, 2009).

[15] James 4:7-8.

[16] Colossians 3:2.

# The Character of God

**God is...**

| | |
|---|---|
| Caring | 1 Peter 5:7 |
| Compassionate | Ps. 111:4, Ps. 145:8, Matt. 14:14, 1 Cor. 1:3 |
| Faithful | Deut. 7:9, Is. 49;7, 1 Cor. 1:9, 1 Cor. 10:13, 1 Thes. 5:24, 1 Thes. 3:3, Heb. 10:23 |
| Forgiving | Ps. 103:3, 1 Jn. 1:9, Lk. 23:34, Eph. 4:32, Col. 3:13 |
| Gentle | Ps. 18:35, Matt. 11:29, Is. 40:11 |
| Giving/Generous/ Provider | Ps. 84:11, James 1:17, Phil. 4:19, Lk. 11:9-13 |
| Good | Ps. 25:8, Ps. 34:8, Ps. 86:5, Ps. 100:5, Ps. 145:9, Lk. 18:19, Nahum 1:7 |
| Holy | Lev. 11:44, Lev. 20:26, 1 Sam. 2:2, Josh. 24:19, Ps. 99:9, 1 Peter 1:16 |
| Honest/Truthful | Num. 23:19, Ps. 31:5, Ps. 33:4, Jn. 17:17, Jn. 8:39-58, Deut. 32:4 |
| Just/Righteous | Zeph. 3:5, Acts 3:14, Ps. 33:5, Dan. 9:14, Rev. 19:2, Is. 45:21, Ex. 9:27, Ezra 9:15, Ps. 119:137-138 |
| Kind | Eph. 2:7, Titus 3:4, Neh. 9:17, Ps. 117:2, Is. 54:8, Joel 2:13 |

| | |
|---|---|
| Longsuffering/Patient | 1 Pet. 3:9, Rom. 15:5, Ex. 34:6, Num. 14:18, Ps. 86:15 |
| Loving/Full of Loving Kindness | Jer. 9:24, Jer. 31:3, Jn. 3:16, Gal. 2:20, Eph. 2:4, 1 Jn. 4:10, Rev. 1:5, Rom. 5:8, Ps. 31:6-8, Ps. 33:5 |
| Merciful | Ps. 111:4, James 5:11, Eph. 2:4-9, Titus 3:3-7 |
| True | Matt. 22:16/Mk. 12:14, Jn. 3:33, Jn. 17:3, Rom. 3:4, Rev. 19:11 |
| Trustworthy | 1 Sam. 22:31, Job 13:15, Ps. 37:3-6 |
| Wise/Giver of Wisdom | Rom. 11:33, Rom. 16:27, 1 Tim. 1:17, Jude 1:25, Dan. 2:20, James 1:5 |

# Hearing God's Voice Outline

My presuppositions for this teaching are:

1) The Bible is God's inspired and authoritative word, and it is true.

2) God created us for the purpose of intimate relationship with him. Our rebellion against him hindered that relationship. According to the Scriptures, receiving Jesus as savior and lord is the only way to be reconciled back into relationship with the Father.

    a. The greatest command is to love God with all (Matt. 22:37), and John 3:16 talks of God's love for us in giving us the gift of his son so we could have eternal life. Eternal life is knowing God and his son (John 17:3). Jesus came so there would be a way back to God's intended purpose for us—intimate friendship with God.

    b. He calls us Friends, James 2:23 and John 15:14; Sons and daughters 2 Cor. 6:18, 1John 3:1-2; Loves the church as a husband should love his wife Eph. 5:25. All these statements imply intimate relationship with those who receive Him as their King.

3) Among beings that have intellect, will, and emotions, *communication* is an essential aspect to truly close, loving, healthy (intimate) relationship. Communication means talking *and* listening - it's two sided. Intimate communication involves honestly sharing thoughts, feelings, dreams, desires, perspective, etc. back and forth.

4) Prayer is Communication/Fellowship w/God Jesus prayed - Luke 5:16; Eph. 6:18 - Exhortation to pray always w/all prayer; Pray without ceasing - 1

Thess. 5:17. How do we do that? Our spirits relating to Him at all times. An awareness of Him with us, and sharing every aspect of our life with Him. I Speak, God listens - Prov. 15:29, Ps. 66:19, Ps. 65:2, Ex. 22:26, 27; God Speaks, I listen and obey if a command is given - John 10:3-4, 14; John 12:49-50

How Does God Speak?

1) Through his Word (Ps. 119:105)
2) Audible voice (Ex. 3:4, Acts 9:1-7)
3) Through others (1 Sam. 3:4 - 19)
4) Through visions (Is. 6:1, Acts 9:10-19, Rev. 1:12-17)
5) Through dreams (Mt. 2:12)
6) (Most commonly) Quiet Inner Voice (Is. 30:21, 1 Kings 19:11-12)
7) Angels (Genesis 16)

Other Scriptures - Acts 8:26-38 - Philip and the Ethiopian; Acts 10:19-20 - Peter on Roof; John 12:49-50 - Jesus did nothing but what the Father showed Him.

"If you know the Lord, you have already heard His voice - it is that inner leading that brought you to Him in the first place...Hearing the voice of the heavenly Father is a basic right of every child of God." (Loren Cunningham, *Is That Really You, God?,* Appendix)

How Do I Hear Him?

1) Spend time just with Him. He's with you always, but we need focused time with Him.
2) Practice listening. The more you do, the easier it will be to recognize when He is speaking to you. "It's actually hard not to hear God if you really want to please and obey Him." (Loren Cunningham, Ibid.)

## How Do I Know If It Is God Speaking To Me?

1) He will never contradict his written word. If what you hear does contradict, it isn't Him.
2) What He says will line up with His character (i.e. good, loving, kind, wise, etc.).
3) What He says will usually be something that inspires you towards Him, not away from Him.

# *Acknowledgements*

Dozens of people helped me become who I am and understand what I understand about God, His character, and His truth principles. I don't have space to thank you all by name. So, out of necessity, listed below are only the key individuals who've played a vital role from the "conception" of this book project to its "birth." To the rest, if you call me friend and have prayed for me, taught me, partnered with me financially, encouraged me, and/or cheered me on to God's purposes for my life, please hear now my very sincere "Thank you!!!" I love and appreciate each of you!

Bill and Oneita McDowell – Dad and Mom, your love, consistency, encouragement, and mentorship have been the biggest earthly influences in me becoming who I am. Thank you for being there for me and partnering with me in multitudes of ways as I do my best to obey God. I'm so honored to be your daughter and your "Princess"! I love you!!!!

Teresa Short – From start to finish, dear friend, you've been with me all the way. When I gave you my attempt at a first chapter and said, "This is conception. Please help me not abort this baby God's put within me," you took me seriously. This book would not exist if you had not encouraged me, prayed fervently, given me your input and simply loved me through the process. Any life ministered to through this book is a life you influenced. Thank you, thank you, thank you for being who you are in my life – a God-given gift of a friend!!! FFAA

Woodcrest Writer's School Friends – Thanks to each person who taught me, listened to me, critiqued my thoughts and ideas about the book and told me I could do it. Special thanks to: Jan Rogers who taught me the basics about communicating through writing; Elaine who actually gave me the name for the book; and my good friend Darlene Harris who prayed for me and gave me some great input when you read the manuscript. I'm truly, truly grateful to each of you!

To those who allowed me to share your stories, (you know who you are), I can't thank you enough. Because of your willingness to be vulnerable to share your failures and what God taught you in the midst of them, many will be inspired to turn to the Lord to set them free from bondage, as well. Only eternity will reveal the extent to which your openness changed lives. It's a privilege to know each of you, and thanks again for helping me make God's point about love needs being best met when we look to Him!

Gillian and Erin – Thanks for your hard work in editing and doing the graphics and layout for the book cover. Without your help this book would be a lot less readable and eye catching. I appreciate everything you did to get the book ready to go to the publisher.

Dean, Maureen, Fran, Pastor Saali, Aaryn, and John H. – Thanks for reading the manuscript and either passing it on to someone else who could endorse it or giving the endorsement yourself. I appreciate you taking the time to read what God gave me to write and liking it enough to encourage others to read it, as well.

To all those who donated toward the publishing of *Love Needs* (you know who you are) – Thanks for asking the Lord if you could partner with me in seeing this "book baby" come forth and then obeying Him when He said yes. May the financial seed you sowed into this project produce much fruit – to the glory of God. Amen!

Marc and Sow The Seed Ministries – It was so nice to make a call and actually talk to a person who helped me and gave me straight answers. Though your company isn't large or well known, you are indeed ministers. Thank you for helping me "birth" this dream of God.

And lastly, but most importantly, thank you Father, Son and Holy Spirit for your love, patience, grace, mercy, anointing, faithfulness, and loving perseverance with me through this whole process. You gave me the insights and inspired me to put them on paper. I can only pray that my best effort to honor You with my love and obedience has put a smile on Your face and will bring You the glory of which You are so worthy. Amen!

Email Deonn for more copies of "Love Needs" or to share any testimonies you have after reading the book:
loveneedsbook@gmail.com